NORTH WALES
>> TRAIL RUNNING
20 OFF-ROAD ROUTES FOR
TRAIL & FELL RUNNERS

Vertebrate Publishing, Sheffield
www.**v-publishing**.c

NORTH WALES
>> TRAIL RUNNING
20 OFF-ROAD ROUTES FOR
TRAIL & FELL RUNNERS

Steve Franklin

NORTH WALES
» TRAIL RUNNING
20 OFF-ROAD ROUTES FOR
TRAIL & FELL RUNNERS

 First published in 2017 by Vertebrate Publishing.

Vertebrate Publishing, Crescent House, 228 Psalter Lane, Sheffield S11 8UT, United Kingdom.
www.v-publishing.co.uk

Front cover: Steve Franklin above Gogarth Bay on the Holyhead Mountain route (run 4).
Back cover: Tony and Sarah Whitehouse overlooked by Tryfan on the Y Foel Goch & Cwm Tryfan route (run 16).
Photography by Keith Sharples unless otherwise credited.

 All maps reproduced by permission of Ordnance Survey
on behalf of The Controller of Her Majesty's Stationery Office.
© Crown Copyright. 100025218.

Design and production by Jane Beagley, Vertebrate Publishing.
www.v-publishing.co.uk

Printed and bound in Europe by Pulsio.

Vertebrate Publishing is committed to printing on paper from sustainable sources.

>> CONTENTS

>> INTRODUCTION

North Wales potentially has the most diverse yet accessible terrain of anywhere in the UK. Only a few minutes' drive from the A55 you can be on sandy shores or mountaintops, or deep in woodland. This variety has to be what makes the area one of the best in the world for all types of adventurer. However, if you want to explore, get away from the crowds and really discover the beauty of North Wales I don't believe there is a better means than on foot. You don't have to be a hard-core fell runner – beard, string vest and three-inch shorts, nor do you need to be kitted head to toe in the latest, most hi-tech and (usually) brightest gear there is. All you really need is an understanding and respect for the area you're in, a sensible choice of clothing and equipment, and a willingness to challenge yourself.

North Wales is made great by its rocky outcrops, large cwms, ridges and steep-sided valleys. This does pose one issue for the novice off-road runner in that it perhaps isn't the friendliest place to learn to run on the fells. Whereas the Peak District and Lake District lend themselves to more logical, shorter and amenable routes, North Wales is a victim of its own awe-inspiring rocky landscape, suffering from fewer short loops around smaller valleys or bodies of water. It's important to remember here that just because a route is short does not mean it is easy; a quick look at the elevation should give a good indication as to how tough the route is.

North Wales has several lifetimes' worth of running adventures and no book could possibly do justice to them all. I've done my best to cover a broad area from as far north as the top of Anglesey, to almost reaching the Welsh-English border and all the way down to Cadair Idris. The majority of routes are located in the heart of Snowdonia; this is not due to them being the best (my personal favourite being Cadair Idris), but more in an effort to provide the most visited area with a wider variety of routes. I sincerely hope the routes slightly further afield will inspire you to venture away from the honeypot areas and discover a place you may never have considered visiting. I've spent years heading down to the Llŷn Peninsula passing Yr Eifl (The Rivals) countless times, always thinking I need to run up there one day; it took this guidebook for me to do it and I am so glad I did. Hopefully this book will give you a similar impetus and you will discover a new favourite summit or view.

I feel it's important to remind you that the mountain environment is inherently dangerous – things can change fast and what was a short run out could become more serious, whether you hurt yourself or a friend hurts themselves, or perhaps you're required to help other mountain users; please be prepared and stay safe.

Steve Franklin

ACKNOWLEDGEMENTS

Thanks to Jon at Vertebrate for asking me to write this guide and to both Jon B and John C for bearing with me while I procrastinated like a champion! Thanks also to Keith Sharples for coming over to Wales several times to take photos and do a bit of running himself. Skip the dog, my trusty running partner, deserves many thanks for sharing the trails with me and helping heat the van on cold winter nights, as does Sarah for venturing over with me time and time again and giving me a helpful nudge when I've been slacking.

I'd also like to thank everyone who has given me a bed in North Wales since I moved back to Sheffield: Nikki, Jim, Alex, Harry and Esther, and anyone else I may have forgotten!

ABOUT THE ROUTES

There is a large contrast in difficulty between the routes. I have done my best in advising how long a route may take, however this is totally subjective and depends on the runner or runners, the state of the trails, the weather and, in a few cases, your ability to navigate using a map and compass.

In addition to the total time I've used **Mountain Goats** and **Navigation** ratings. **Mountain Goats** is on a scale of 🐐 (easy), 🐐 🐐 (medium) and 🐐 🐐 🐐 (hard), and **Navigation** is rated on a scale from from 1 (easy) to 5 (hard).

For example:

A route graded **Mountain Goats** 🐐 and **Navigation** 1 will generally be on good paths and tracks and should be easy to navigate in most weather conditions.

A route graded **Mountain Goats** 🐐 🐐 and **Navigation** 1 will be on terrain that is more technical. This may mean it is rocky, loose or muddy or that there is a lot of ascent and descent (or both), but there are plenty of waymarkers to look out for and the paths are still easy to recognise and follow.

A route graded **Mountain Goats** 🐐 🐐 🐐 and **Navigation** 5 indicates that the terrain is very difficult. Possibly covering open fell with no paths or tracks, very steep ground, and on loose, slippery and muddy terrain. Additionally the route may also be more committing, being further from roads or without mobile phone reception. With regards to navigation there are likely to be sections of the route which are without waymarkers and obvious features, making the ability to use a map and compass essential. On top of this, errors in navigation may be costly, leading you hours from your start point.

MAPS

All the routes are carefully described and plotted on Ordnance Survey 1:25,000 mapping, but it is strongly recommended that you carry the relevant full map and a compass. **Explorers OL17, OL18, OL23, 254, 262, 263, 264** and **265** cover all the runs in this guide and are essential even if you are familiar with the area – you may need to cut short a run or take an alternative route. And of course, a map is no use without the navigational skills to use it.

DESCRIPTIONS, DISTANCES & ASCENT

While every effort has been made to ensure accuracy within the maps and descriptions in this guide, we are unable to guarantee that every single detail is correct. Please exercise caution if a direction appears at odds with the route on the ground. If in doubt, a comparison between the directions, map and a bit of common sense should ensure you're on the right track.

Distances are in kilometres and height gain is in metres. Both were measured using GPS devices on the runs, but we cannot promise that they are 100 per cent accurate, so please treat stated distances as a guideline only. Our estimated times are a combination of optimism, generosity, challenge and fiction; just allow plenty of time and try to run an even pace.

Ordnance Survey maps are the most commonly used, are easy to read and many people are happy using them. If you're not familiar with OS maps and are unsure of what the symbols mean, you can download a free OS 1:25,000 map legend from **www.ordnancesurvey.co.uk**

Here are a few of the symbols and abbreviations we use on the maps and in our directions:

 ROUTE STARTING POINT   ROUTE MARKER

 OPTIONAL ROUTE   ADDITIONAL GRID LINE NUMBERS TO AID NAVIGATION

TERRAIN

I've done my utmost to give accurate descriptions of the land, waymarkers and surroundings. I've not asked you to turn right at the red tractor – however, it's important to remember that even relatively permanent features can change. Maps can go out of date quickly, footpaths can be rerouted, woodland can be felled, rivers can swell and signposts can be moved. The weather before you head out on your run can also dramatically alter the state of the route, in particular those on open fells and less-distinct paths. They may become even less obvious, or unrunnably (this has to be a word) muddy.

WHAT'S YOUR
MOUNTOPIA?

Day 195. Pascal Egli's Mountopia – Dolomites Skyrace on 1st place.

Reach your Mountopia with **dynafit.com**

Concept and Design Pescher+Heinz, Photo KME Studios – Michael Müller

GORE-TEX

Official Partner

Dynafit trail running now available
at V12 Outdoor, Llanberis

RECOMMENDED EQUIPMENT

Recommended kit varies depending on the time of year and the difficulty and nature of the route. While many runners like the freedom of a 'fast and light' approach, longer and more remote runs are best undertaken with a little more kit.

» **Bag:** there are plenty of lightweight rucksacks and bumbags on the market. Find one that's comfy and doesn't move around on rough ground.
» **Waterproofs/windproofs:** jacket and trousers. We'd strongly recommend fully waterproof with taped seams, this is Snowdonia and North Wales.
» **Hat and gloves:** keep your extremities warm and the rest will follow. It's no fun fumbling with shoelaces with frozen fingers.
» **Map and compass:** and know how to use them! The relevant maps are listed on page X.
» **Whistle:** six short blasts in quick succession means 'help!'
» **Space blanket and small first aid kit:** weigh nothing, take up hardly any room and could save your life.
» **Food and water:** enough for your expected duration of the run and some emergency rations.
» **Headtorch:** if you're heading out late, a headtorch should be high on your list of essentials.

LOOKING ACROSS LLYN PADARN TO THE LLANBERIS PASS

FOOTWEAR

We recommend at least 'trail' shoes for all these routes, with fell shoes being desirable on the harder routes. Trail shoes offer more grip and greater stability than road shoes, while the deep lugs on the soles of fell shoes will come in handy on boggy or wet ground.

CLOTHING

Dress appropriately for the season. Shorts and a vest work well on hot summer days, but thermals, windproofs and gloves are better on winter runs. Please note that exposure on higher ground is a very real risk for the tired, lost or slowing runner – better to carry a small bag with full waterproofs and gloves/hat, than be flapping around on the top of Snowdon trying to get a signal and call out mountain rescue.

FUEL & HYDRATION

Hot days can be deadly for the trail runner. We don't recommend drinking from any streams in North Wales, so carry sufficient water (either in bottles or a hydration pack) for your run. Likewise, a banana or two and an 'emergency' gel can come in handy, especially on long days out.

SAFETY

Ideally, run in pairs, tell someone where you are going and carry a phone – but note that finding good reception is difficult in many parts of Snowdonia and North Wales. Should you find yourself out of reception, be grateful to be temporarily free of the phone's tyranny.

MOUNTAIN RESCUE

In case of an accident or similar requiring mountain rescue assistance, dial 999 and ask for **POLICE – MOUNTAIN RESCUE**. Be prepared to give a 6-figure grid reference of your position in the case of a mountain location.

MOUNTAIN RESCUE BY SMS TEXT

Another option in the UK is contacting the emergency services by SMS text – useful if you have a low battery or intermittent signal. You need to register first – text 'register' to 999 and then follow the instructions in the reply. **www.emergencysms.org.uk**

THE COUNTRYSIDE CODE
RESPECT OTHER PEOPLE

Please respect the local community and other people using the outdoors. Remember your actions can affect people's lives and livelihoods.

Consider the local community and other people enjoying the outdoors

» Respect the needs of local people and visitors alike – for example, don't block gateways, driveways or other paths with your vehicle.

» When riding a bike or driving a vehicle, slow down or stop for horses, walkers and farm animals and give them plenty of room. By law, cyclists must give way to walkers and horse riders on bridleways.

» Co-operate with people at work in the countryside. For example, keep out of the way when farm animals are being gathered or moved and follow directions from the farmer.

» Busy traffic on small country roads can be unpleasant and dangerous to local people, visitors and wildlife – so slow down and, where possible, leave your vehicle at home, consider sharing lifts and use alternatives such as public transport or cycling. For public transport information, phone Traveline on **0871 200 22 33** or visit **www.traveline.info**

Leave gates and property as you find them and follow paths unless wider access is available

» A farmer will normally close gates to keep farm animals in, but may sometimes leave them open so the animals can reach food and water. Leave gates as you find them or follow instructions on signs. When in a group, make sure the last person knows how to leave the gates.

» Follow paths unless wider access is available, such as on open country or registered common land (known as 'open access' land).

» If you think a sign is illegal or misleading such as a *Private – No Entry* sign on a public path, contact the local authority.

» Leave machinery and farm animals alone – don't interfere with animals even if you think they're in distress. Try to alert the farmer instead.

» Use gates, stiles or gaps in field boundaries if you can – climbing over walls, hedges and fences can damage them and increase the risk of farm animals escaping.

» Our heritage matters to all of us – be careful not to disturb ruins and historic sites.

PROTECT THE NATURAL ENVIRONMENT

We all have a responsibility to protect the countryside now and for future generations, so make sure you don't harm animals, birds, plants or trees and try to leave no trace of your visit. When out with your dog make sure it is not a danger or nuisance to farm animals, horses, wildlife or other people.

Leave no trace of your visit and take your litter home

» Protecting the natural environment means taking special care not to damage, destroy or remove features such as rocks, plants and trees. They provide homes and food for wildlife, and add to everybody's enjoyment of the countryside.

» Litter and leftover food doesn't just spoil the beauty of the countryside, it can be dangerous to wildlife and farm animals – so take your litter home with you. Dropping litter and dumping rubbish are criminal offences.

» Fires can be as devastating to wildlife and habitats as they are to people and property – so be careful with naked flames and cigarettes at any time of the year. Sometimes, controlled fires are used to manage vegetation, particularly on heaths and moors between 1 October and 15 April, but if a fire appears to be unattended then report it by calling **999**.

Keep dogs under effective control

When you take your dog into the outdoors, always ensure it does not disturb wildlife, farm animals, horses or other people by keeping it under effective control. This means that you:

» keep your dog on a lead, or

» keep it in sight at all times, be aware of what it's doing and be confident it will return to you promptly on command

» ensure it does not stray off the path or area where you have a right of access

Special dog rules may apply in particular situations, so always look out for local signs – for example:

» dogs may be banned from certain areas that people use, or there may be restrictions, byelaws or control orders limiting where they can go

» the access rights that normally apply to open country and registered common land (known as 'open access' land) require dogs to be kept on a short lead between 1 March and 31 July, to help protect ground-nesting birds, and all year round near farm animals

» at the coast, there may also be some local restrictions to require dogs to be kept on a short lead during the bird breeding season, and to prevent disturbance to flocks of resting and feeding birds during other times of year

It's always good practice (and a legal requirement on 'open access' land) to keep your dog on a lead around farm animals and horses, for your own safety and for the welfare of the animals. A farmer may shoot a dog which is attacking or chasing farm animals without being liable to compensate the dog's owner.

However, if cattle or horses chase you and your dog, it is safer to let your dog off the lead – don't risk getting hurt by trying to protect it. Your dog will be much safer if you let it run away from a farm animal in these circumstances and so will you.

Everyone knows how unpleasant dog mess is and it can cause infections, so always clean up after your dog and get rid of the mess responsibly – 'bag it and bin it'. Make sure your dog is wormed regularly to protect it, other animals and people.

ENJOY THE OUTDOORS

Even when going out locally, it's best to get the latest information about where and when you can go. For example, your rights to go on to some areas of open access land and coastal land may be restricted in particular places at particular times. Find out as much as you can about where you are going, plan ahead and follow advice and local signs.

Plan ahead and be prepared

You'll get more from your visit if you refer to up-to-date maps or guidebooks and websites before you go. Visit **www.gov.uk/natural-england** or contact local information centres or libraries for a list of outdoor recreation groups offering advice on specialist activities.

You're responsible for your own safety and for others in your care – especially children – so be prepared for natural hazards, changes in weather and other events. Wild animals, farm animals and horses can behave unpredictably if you get too close, especially if they're with their young – so give them plenty of space.

Check weather forecasts before you leave. Conditions can change rapidly especially on mountains and along the coast, so don't be afraid to turn back. When visiting the coast check for tide times on **www.ukho.gov.uk/easytide** – don't risk getting cut off by rising tides and take care on slippery rocks and seaweed.

Part of the appeal of the countryside is that you can get away from it all. You may not see anyone for hours, and there are many places without clear mobile phone signals, so let someone else know where you're going and when you expect to return.

Follow advice and local signs

England has about 190,000 km (118,000 miles) of public rights of way, providing many opportunities to enjoy the natural environment. Get to know the signs and symbols used in the countryside to show paths and open countryside.

LODGE

DINORWIG

THE BEST INCENTIVE TO RUN UP THAT HILL

01286 - 871632

CAFE & 4* HOSTEL
OPEN ALL YEAR ROUND

BREAKFAST	DINORWIG
LUNCH	CAERNARFON
COFFEE	GWYNEDD
CAKE	LL55 3EY

CONTAINS ORDNANCE SURVEY DATA © CROWN COPYRIGHT AND DATABASE RIGHT.

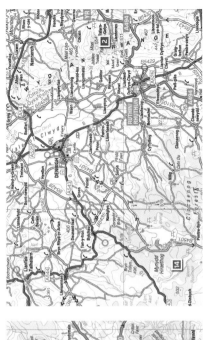

NORTH WALES TRAIL RUNNING
AREA MAP
>> MAP

THE
TRAILS

Some routes in this guide will be an acquired taste. For those that like it so steep you need to put your hands to your knees and fell-walk away there are routes for you; for those that want to take in summit after summit there are routes for you; for those who are new to off-road running there are routes for you.

I've no doubt that there will be those who wonder why I didn't include certain routes or summits and why I have included others. However, I do believe there is a wonderful range of routes with a plethora of different characteristics and locations to suit all types of runner and outdoor enthusiast alike.

LOOKING DOWN INTO CWM IDWAL FROM THE GLYDERS

INTRODUCTION

The Ogwen valley and Cwm Idwal are famed for their glacial rock formations and rare flora and fauna, and in 1954 Cwm Idwal became Wales's first Natural Nature Reserve. This route takes you up into the cwm, an environment more akin to the high mountains. Llyn Idwal is encircled by the Glyderau range; Glyder Fach, Glyder Fawr and Y Garn dominate the cwm to the south and west, and the serrated summit of Tryfan, one of the most recognisable mountains in Great Britain, stands proud to the east. If you look carefully at the summit you'll spot two monoliths – Adam and Eve. It is tradition to leap the gap between the two monoliths, but this isn't for the faint-hearted! This stunning backdrop is home to the perfect entry-level trail run, which explores this wild environment in relative safety.

THE ROUTE

After a gentle climb to the llyn from Ogwen Cottage, the route passes below the infamous Idwal Slabs, a rock face used by some of Britain's most famous climbers. Further on and higher up the hillside a gaping chasm becomes apparent – this is Twll Du, or the Devil's Kitchen. There's an optional extension to this which adds on a tricky river crossing and some technical terrain. While the area feels wild and remote, it is relatively safe as the route stays low and sheltered. As the route returns along the western flank of Llyn Idwal the grandeur of the Nant Ffrancon valley becomes apparent. A text-book example of glaciation from the last Ice Age; it's almost possible to imagine the glacier scooping out the sides of the valley to leave the classic U-shape.

Note that while this route is on well-trodden and clear paths, they are rocky so there is some technical aspect to the running.

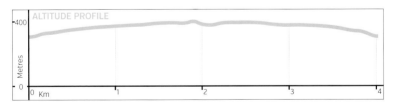

ALTITUDE PROFILE

>> LLYN IDWAL LOOP

DISTANCE 4KM >> *ASCENT* 100M >> *TYPICAL TIME* 0:30–1:00 HRS >> *TERRAIN* TRAIL >> *NAVIGATION* 1 – STRAIGHTFORWARD, TAKE CARE ON THE FINAL DESCENT TO OGWEN COTTAGE >> *START/FINISH* PAY & DISPLAY CAR PARK BY OGWEN COTTAGE >> *GRID REF* SH 650603 >> *SATNAV* LL57 3LZ >> *OS MAP* EXPLORER OL17 SNOWDON >> *TRANSPORT* BUSES FROM BETHESDA AND BETWS-Y-COED >> *REFRESHMENTS* CAFE [SEASONAL], TOILETS & INFORMATION CENTRE AT OGWEN COTTAGE

S From Ogwen Cottage, head along the main path to the walkers' path **left** of the information centre, shortly passing through a gate and over a large bridge. At the junction **bear right** on to the flagstoned path heading gently uphill towards the llyn.

2 **Turn left** at the llyn down the eastern shore with the water on your right. Pass through a stone wall and swing gate. To your right is a small island, the vegetation growing here is potentially what the entire valley may look like in years to come as grazing animals are no longer allowed beyond the stone wall. Continue around the llyn to reach the foot of the Idwal Slabs, the large leaning rock face at the head of the llyn.

3 Head beneath the slabs. Past the slabs, **turn right*** keeping near to the water's edge. **Keep bearing right**, passing an old sheep pen and eventually reaching a junction.

*OPTIONAL ROUTE

▶ OR ▷ If you wish to see the Devil's Kitchen, **keep left** here and follow the path around the head of the cwm. Rejoin the route at point 4.

4 **Turn right** again, along the western shore of the lake. Just before the gate through the stone wall, go over the stile on your **left**, crossing a fence. Follow the faint and uneven grass path north, very gently losing height. The path becomes much more worn and rutted. It drops steeply for a short distance before you cross a wall and stone stile into a narrow gorge with high, rocky sides. **Take care** as the rock can be slippy. Continue through the gorge for a short distance before arriving back at Ogwen Cottage.

THE VIEW ACROSS TO SNOWDON FROM THE GLYDERS

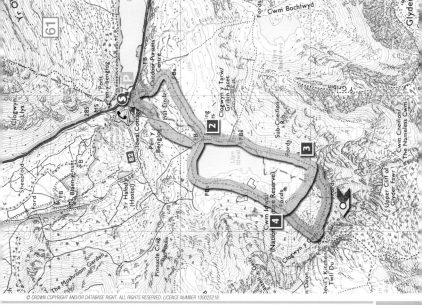

INTRODUCTION

A brief foray into the wonderful Clwydian Hills. The running is good and the views are even better. If the weather has been kind you'll be able to see as far as Snowdon. On the summit of Moel Famau you'll find the Jubilee Tower, built in 1810 to commemorate the Golden Jubilee of George III. Due to funds the tower was never fully completed and in 1862 a major storm brought it down. It lay in ruins until 1969 when the remains of the fallen tower were cleared leaving the lower tier which is still standing today.

THE ROUTE

This run is on well-trodden and easy-to-follow paths for its entirety. The route has some steep sections but in the main is an enjoyable and accessible route for all runners.

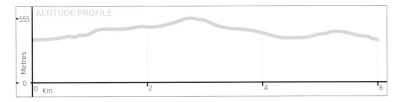

ALTITUDE PROFILE

555

Metres

0

0 Km   2   4   6

» MOEL FAMAU

DISTANCE 6KM » *ASCENT* 185M » *TYPICAL TIME* 0:45–1:15 HRS » *TERRAIN* TRAIL » *NAVIGATION* 1 – VERY EASY, COULD BE DONE IN POOR VISIBILITY » *START/FINISH* BWLCH PENBARRAS CAR PARK, 2KM NORTH-EAST OF LLANBEDR-DYFFRYN-CLWYD » *GRID REF* SJ 161605 » *SATNAV* CH7 5SH [NEAREST] » *OS MAP* EXPLORER 265 CLWYDIAN RANGE » *REFRESHMENTS* VARIOUS OPTIONS IN RUTHIN; PUBLIC TOILETS AT LOWER [EASTERN] CAR PARK

DIRECTIONS » MOEL FAMAU

S   Park in the car park on the northern side of the road. Head past the large wooden gate and follow the sign for *Jubilee Tower*. Stay on the wide track as it gradually gains height. The track draws level with a large stone wall. Just before reaching the Jubilee Tower it steepens.

2   From the summit retrace your steps for 50m back down the steep path. Take the **left** turn, indicated by the blue arrow on the wooden post. Go through a gate and, just after, at the junction, **bear left** and **right** dropping steeply downhill on a good track. Continue downhill, entering the woodland, passing a large fallen tree. **Continue ahead** until you reach a crossroads junction.

3   **Turn right** at the junction on to a narrower path. As the path opens out at the next junction follow the red arrows to your **right**, leading around two small ponds. Exit on to the fire road and **turn right**. Continue gently uphill and as the path forks **bear left** on the wider track, climbing gradually. Follow this back to the car park.

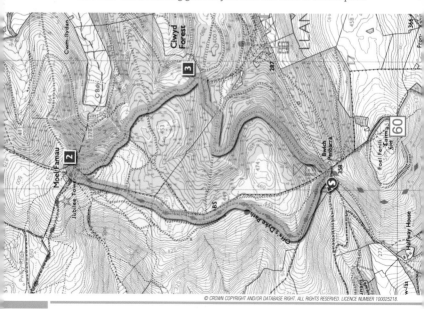

INTRODUCTION

Steeped in history and boasting some of the best and most accessible views in North Wales, Conwy Mountain has to be one of the most looked-at but least-frequented hills in North Wales. Only a stone's throw from the A55, the number of tourists sat in bank holiday traffic who will have crawled past and looked up at the steep northern flanks of Conwy Mountain (Mynydd y Dref) and thought they should head up there one day but have never bothered to take the five-minute detour are all missing out. From the top of the mountain you get the most amazing panoramas of the Ormes, Anglesey and obviously Snowdonia. Not only are the views second to none but the hill is rich in history – on the summit you'll find Neolithic hut circles and an Iron Age hill fort.

THE ROUTE

This route is a great introduction to off-road running, with a combination of wide-open tracks and a few short-lived more technical sections. Part of the route is made up of the 97-kilometre North Wales Path, with a minor detour to the summit of Allt Wen on some fantastically fun singletrack to drop you off back at the Sychnant Pass.

Despite the ease of access and proximity to the A55 the mountain never seems to be busy and it's a great way to get some miles in if you've only got an evening before or after a long drive, or if you're heading home and want to sneak in one last run.

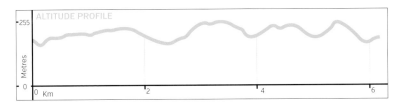

ALTITUDE PROFILE

255 / 0 Metres · 0 Km · 2 · 4 · 6

» CONWY MOUNTAIN

DISTANCE 6.2KM » **ASCENT** 252M » **TYPICAL TIME** 1:00–1:30 HRS » **TERRAIN** PATHS/TRODS » **NAVIGATION** 2 – SOME NAVIGATIONAL SKILLS ARE REQUIRED, ESPECIALLY IN BAD VISIBILITY. THE QUARRIED NATURE OF CONWY MOUNTAIN MEANS THERE ARE CLIFF FACES AND LARGE DROPS » **START/FINISH** FREE PARKING EITHER SIDE OF THE ROAD, SYCHNANT PASS SUMMIT. SPACE FOR 10 CARS » **GRID REF** SH 749770 » **SATNAV** LL32 8BJ (NEAREST) » **OS MAP** EXPLORER OL17 SNOWDON » **REFRESHMENTS** CAFES IN CONWY TOWN

DIRECTIONS >> CONWY MOUNTAIN

S From the car park head north up a steep tarmac track with a small rocky outcrop on your right. Keep on this broad track to cross a small river at a ford. Go through the gate and continue **straight ahead** on the dirt track until you reach a small pond on your right.

2 Bear right at the pond and continue on the dirt road with the wall on your right. After 400m take the path **trending left** away from the wall and gently uphill. As the path widens, another path joins from your left. **Turn right** and follow this downhill passing the 'Castell Caer Seion' noticeboard. Keep your eyes peeled for the very large stacked stones on your left and an 'out-of-place' deciduous tree just after. These mark your turn-around point. **Turn left** and **left again** on to a narrow, steep track rising up to the Conwy Mountain summit. The sea should now be on your right.

3 Climb Conwy Mountain to reach the trig point and take the obvious path off the western side. Descend steeply for 400m before reaching a plateau. Continue **straight ahead** on the good path, passing a bench on your right. Just beyond the bench **trend right** and uphill on a wide grassy path, shortly reaching another wide dirt track. Carry on **straight ahead** until you reach a large sheep pen.

4 Follow the wall of the sheep pen, **straight ahead** at first then **turning left**. At the north-western corner of the wall continue **straight ahead** on an obvious path towards a lone spruce tree. Stay on the main track, descending gently and bearing **leftwards** until you reach another larger stone wall. Handrail this as it goes up a steep bank before taking the obvious path from the wall corner. Stay on this for 50m before there is a **sharp right** turn cutting back on yourself. Take this.

5 The path runs beneath and then to the right of three very obvious and slightly out-of-place large boulders. Climb steeply up the track and as you crest the summit (the walls of the old fort) go **straight ahead** along the plateau before reaching the summit proper. **Trend leftwards** and continue on the path dropping down steeply. When given the option, **bear right**, back towards the car park. The path rejoins the main track you started out on at the top of the tarmac section – retrace your steps beneath the large rocky outcrops to the car park.

STEVE FRANKLIN DESCENDING FROM ALLT WEN

FINE RUNNING ABOVE THE MAIN CLIFF OF GOGARTH

6.4km

INTRODUCTION

Holyhead Mountain lies on the north-westernmost tip of Wales, on the island of Anglesey. The mountain itself stands proud as you drive north-west, its rocky summit dominating the skyline. The exposed sea cliffs hereabouts are a haven for wildlife and a magnet for rock climbers, and make for a dramatic and undulating run which circumnavigates the mountain.

If you've got the energy left at the end, it's well worth the run along the shore to the breakwater for a longer-than-expected out and back. The longest breakwater in the UK, it feels remarkably remote.

THE ROUTE

The route starts by passing beneath the old quarry walls above Porth Namarch. The main climb of the route is on good paths but starts steeply, rising above the sea cliffs.

Once the path levels out there is an option to visit the old fog signal station. It's possible to grasp the sheer size of the cliffs around you from the station, however there's a steep haul back up to the main path.

From here, take care to stick to the main path. You'll shortly see why! As you descend off the Wales Coast Path look over your right shoulder and the towering Main Cliff of Gogarth is visible. The last thing you want to do is accidentally run off the top. From here the path remains easily runnable, with a few short inclines. The route takes an about turn at the South Stack lighthouse, heading back towards Holyhead Mountain and con-touring around the rocks; although you don't summit it's easy to take a short detour. The descent back down to the country park is short and sharp, taking some lovely singletrack paths.

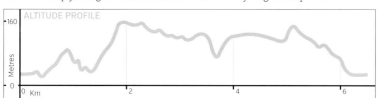

ALTITUDE PROFILE
160
Metres
0
0 Km   2   4   6

>> **HOLYHEAD MOUNTAIN**

DISTANCE 6.4KM >> *ASCENT* 323M >> *TYPICAL TIME* : 0:45-1:15 HRS >> *TERRAIN* PATHS/TRODS >> *NAVIGATION* 1 – PATHS ARE EASY TO FOLLOW AND WELL SIGNPOSTED. ALTHOUGH THE RUN DOESN'T GO TOO NEAR ANY CLIFF EDGES IT IS WORTH BEING CAUTIOUS >> *START/FINISH* PAY & DISPLAY CAR PARK AT BREAKWATER COUNTRY PARK >> *GRID REF* SH 226832 >> *SATNAV* LL65 1YG >> *OS MAP* EXPLORER 262 ANGLESEY WEST >> *TRANSPORT* TRAINS TO HOLYHEAD AND BUSES FROM HOLYHEAD TO THE COUNTRY PARK >> *REFRESHMENTS* CAFE, INFORMATION CENTRE AND PUBLIC TOILETS AT COUNTRY PARK. SOUTH STACK HAS THE SAME AMENITIES AND AN RSPB CENTRE

Gogarth Bay

North Stack/
Ynys Arw

Caves

Parliament House

Cave

Caves

Cave

Cave

Porth
Namarch

Holyhead Breakwater C
Parc Gwledig Morglaw

Mountain
Cottage

Caer y Twr
fort

Holyhead Mountain/
Mynydd Twr

220

South Stack Cliffs
Nature Reserve

Gorlan

MH & MLW

Radio
Stations

Foel

Resr

Quarry
(dis)

Castell

Ffynnon y Wrach
(well)

Stack/
Lawd

FB

Goferydd

Cytiau'r Gwyddelod
(settlement)

Tan-y-cytiau

Twr

Gors-y-twr

Tre-Wilmot

Ellin's
Tower

SEABIRD
CENTRE

Plas
Nicol

Ty'n-nant

Ty-mawr

Pen-las Rock

Henborth

Pillar

Pen-y-bonc

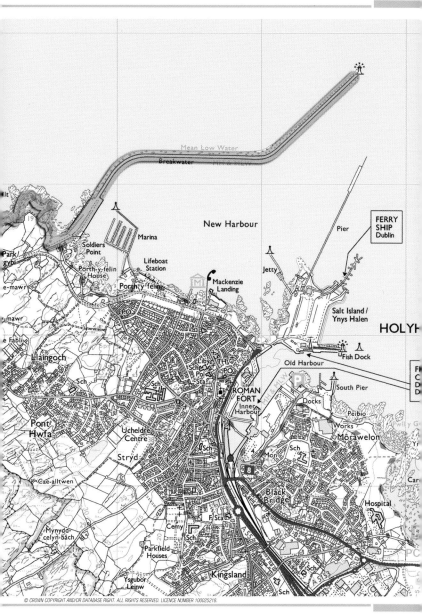

S From the car park follow the signs to *South Stacks*. Side-step through the fence and **turn left** on to the gravel path. After a few metres take a **gentle right** through a large wooden swing gate across a grassy field. Run across the field. After you pass beneath the quarry follow the path around and **left**, uphill. Stay on the well-paved but narrow path, passing an odd-shaped derelict building on your right. Continue **straight ahead** until you reach a major path. **Turn right** on to this.

OPTIONAL ROUTE

If you wish to add on an additional loop and visit the lighthouse **bear right** again, downhill. This path loops back around, climbing steeply; as the path levels take a **sharp right** turn back on yourself.

2 At the next fork **bear left** and **left again**, heading uphill. Keep climbing on the narrow path, crossing an old wall line just before reaching a plateau and the remains of old buildings. As you head off the plateau go **straight ahead**, descending steeply before reaching a crossroads in a flat area. **Turn right** gently uphill to reach the turn for the copa (summit) marked on the wooden post. If you feel inclined the out and back is another great add-on. If not, continue **straight ahead**, downhill. Join the major track and **keep right**.

3 As you run beneath the fenced-off building take the narrow path heading up and **right** to join the tarmac. **Turn left** followed by a **quick right** back on to the singletrack through the brush. Stay on this, descending initially, then climb up to the old telegraph pole. Head straight off the summit down to the road; **turn left**. Pass the benches on your left and a few metres after the sign to *Mynydd Twr* take the narrow path heading up on to the faint ridge. Keep on this to reach a major track and **turn right**. At the major crossroads go **straight ahead**, towards the right-hand side of Holyhead Mountain rocks. Keep on the paths heading in this direction.

4 Once you're beneath the right-hand end of the rocks take a narrow path on your **left**, which leads uphill and gently to the right before bearing back left to take you over the shoulder of Holyhead Mountain. **Ignore** all the minor trods which lead off the main path. Continue until you reach a wall on your right; this soon becomes a corridor with walls on both sides. Descend more steeply until you reach a lane head and tarmac road.

5   **Turn left**, back on to the grassy path for a short distance before reaching another road. Follow the road gently downhill passing by a house with a large stone front before reaching another grassy track. This turns into gravel and is interspersed with steep steps which lead you back down into the country park.

OPTIONAL ROUTE

OR   If you've still got some beans left there is a delightful out and back to the end of the breakwater. Head back to the start of the run, side-stepping through the fence again but this time go straight on, down towards the sea. The path runs along the coastline for around 1.6km before reaching the breakwater. Don't be deceived, the breakwater is longer than it looks and from end to end is 2.4km.

MAIN CLIFF, GOGARTH

05 » LLYN PADARN LOOP   8.5km

INTRODUCTION

The Llanberis local's evening run; a delightful loop of the llyn on good paths and tracks. Alas it isn't all flat – there are some gentle climbs through the quarries and Allt Wen woods.

THE ROUTE

The Llyn Padarn Loop is proof that you don't have to be a mountain climber or adventurer to enjoy the delights of Snowdonia. Convenience isn't the only reason locals snatch this loop when they're short of time. The views as you head along the southern border of the lake are breathtaking: the chasm that is the Llanberis Pass lies ahead, flanked on the left by the Glyders and on the right by Snowdon. Padarn itself leads you towards the delightfully perched, cylindrical building of Dolbadarn Castle (a slight detour can be easily taken at the southern tip of the llyn to visit the castle; it's possible to enter the castle and view Llanberis Pass from the keep). During busy periods there'll likely be people milling around the Llanberis slate museum and Lake Railway, however as you pass through here you'll find solace in Allt Wen woods as few of the museum goers seem to venture any further than the main attractions. The trails through the woods are wonderful; much thinner and more technical than those on the southern bank but never too steep or tricky.

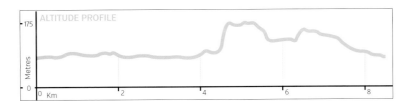

ALTITUDE PROFILE

Metres — 175 / 0

Km — 0, 2, 4, 6, 8

» LLYN PADARN LOOP

DISTANCE 8.5KM » **ASCENT** 140M » **TYPICAL TIME** 1:00 HR » **TERRAIN** ROAD/FIRE ROAD, TRAIL » **NAVIGATION** 1 – REQUIRES LITTLE NAVIGATIONAL EXPERIENCE. PATHS ARE WELL KEPT AND CAN BE RUN IN ROAD OR TRAIL SHOES. MOST TURNS ARE CLEAR AND FREQUENTLY SIGNPOSTED » **START/FINISH** ROADSIDE PARKING JUST SOUTH OF THE BRIDGE AT THE NORTH-WESTERN TIP OF LLYN PADARN » **GRID REF** SH 559623 » **SATNAV** LL55 4EE (NEAREST) » **OS MAP** EXPLORER OL17 SNOWDON » **TRANSPORT** BUS TO LLANBERIS FROM BANGOR » **REFRESHMENTS** REFRESHMENTS: LODGE DINORWIG TEL: 01286 871 632; CAFFI CABAN, BRYNREFAIL TEL: 01286 685 500; VARIOUS IN LLANBERIS VILLAGE

DIRECTIONS » LLYN PADARN LOOP

S Head off anti-clockwise around the lake, going immediately through a gate. After 200m continue through another gate and **turn right**. **Take care** as you cross the A4086. Go through the gate on the other side of the road and **turn left** towards the tunnels. Continue **straight ahead**.

2 Just after going underneath an old iron bridge **bear left**, keeping close to the water's edge. The path winds its way through a picnic area before bringing you back to the pavement. Continue on the pavement for 300m. On reaching a long thin car park take the path which runs just a few metres from the lake. Head towards the playground and **keep left**.

3 Run along the wooden boardwalks to the left of the playground. If dry*, **bear left** crossing the floodplain fields towards the bridge between Llyn Padarn and Llyn Peris.

*OPTIONAL ROUTE

▶ OR If the fields are waterlogged **trend right** on a footpath behind a large building. This will bring you to the railway; do not cross the railway but follow it on its left until you reach the bridge.

4 Cross the bridge and **turn left** on to the road. As you enter the car park **keep right**, cross the railway lines (carefully) at the station cafe. **Turn immediately left** going between two buildings, passing a post with a red and blue sign.

5 Head beneath a large incline and drop down the slate steps, follow the red sign on the wooden post going uphill. As you pass the visitor centre on the switchback, go through the gap in the wall on the apex of the bend. Follow the green arrows on wooden posts. Keep on the high path and don't take any of the small paths which appear to drop down to the lake. As the path starts to bear right around the hillside it also begins to descend steeply down to a large stone bridge.

6 From the bridge take the wide track **straight ahead** uphill (very steep at times) passing frequent white posts. As the road turns sharply right continue **straight ahead** up a short and steep footpath to reach the road. **Turn left** on the road and follow this gently downhill back to the bridge at the tip of Llyn Padarn.

06 >> SNOWDON: LLYN LLYDAW   8.5km

INTRODUCTION

This loop is fantastic, taking in some high mountain scenery without masses of climbing to get there. It can be busy during the day but makes a wonderful outing early in the morning or later in the evening once the hordes have gone home.

THE ROUTE

An exceptionally scenic run up high with varied views throughout. As you set off along the Pyg Track the Llanberis Pass and Llyn Peris are the first sights to catch your eye, with the lake shimmering at the far end of the valley. As you crest Bwlch y Moch and enter the cwm of the Snowdon Horseshoe, Y Lliwedd stands proud opposite with its summit and striking ridgeline running up to the top of Snowdon (Yr Wyddfa). The path rises gently along the flanks of the cwm towards the back wall and the Trinity Face, but the route does not summit Snowdon and instead drops down to the Glaslyn lake from the junction with the Miners' Track. The about-turn opens up another vista and the cwm seems to pour out into the Gwynant valley with the distinct peak of Moel Siabod dominating the skyline. The path descends gradually to reach the shores of Llyn Llydaw before skirting around the llyn and crossing via the causeway, one of the many remnants from the extensive copper mining that was conducted here during the eighteenth and nineteenth centuries.

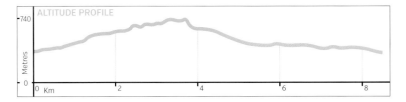

ALTITUDE PROFILE

Metres

>> SNOWDON: LLYN LLYDAW

DISTANCE 8.5KM >> *ASCENT* 305M >> *TYPICAL TIME* 1:00–1:30 HRS >> *TERRAIN* PATHS/TRODS >> *NAVIGATION* 1 – EASILY NAVIGABLE BUT DUE TO THE EXPOSED AND HIGH NATURE IT SHOULDN'T BE TAKEN LIGHTLY >> *START/FINISH* PEN-Y-PASS CAR PARK >> *GRID REF* SH 647556 >> *SATNAV* LL55 4NY >> *OS MAP* EXPLORER OL17 SNOWDON >> *TRANSPORT* REGULAR BUSES FROM LLANBERIS >> *REFRESHMENTS* CAFE AND TOILETS AT THE PEN-Y-PASS CAR PARK

S   From the car park head towards the cafe and take the slabbed path just up and **left**, passing through a gap in the stone wall, signed *Llwybr Pyg Track*. The path is clear and easy to follow all the way to the crest of the ridge at Bwlch y Moch.

2   Continue **straight ahead**, trending **gently right**. The path descends gradually for a short distance before rising up along the northern flanks of the cwm. Stay on this path until you reach the junction with the Miners' Track.

3   **Turn left** down the Miners' Track. At this point you should be descending down towards lake Glaslyn. If you're still climbing then you're en route to the summit. Pass Glaslyn and descend steeply once more before reaching the shores of Llyn Llydaw.

4   Follow the path around the northern shore to reach the causeway. Cross the causeway and follow the wide path as it trends leftwards, past the pipelines on your right. Carry on past the third and smallest llyn in the cwm, Llyn Teyrn. Keep on this path until you arrive back at the car park.

AMY UNDERWOOD THOMPSON ON THE BEDDGELERT FOREST SINGLETRACK

8.7km

INTRODUCTION

Moel yr Ogof and its sister peak Moel Lefn are often overlooked, lying slightly further afield from the main bulk of Snowdonia. They're flanked by the popular and rightly classic Nantlle Ridge to the north and by the dominating Moel Hebog (782 metres) to the south. The bwlchs either side (Bwlch Cwm-trwsgl and Bwlch Meillionen) are two of the easiest routes to access the hidden Cwm Pennant. Combining this with the trails of Beddgelert Forest makes an excellent introduction to fell running.

THE ROUTE

This run is a combination of great trails and open fell with spectacular views of the hidden gem, Cwm Pennant. There'll definitely be the need to walk parts of the route, in particular the climb from Bwlch Cwm-Trwsgl up on to the northern bank

of Moel Lefn and, similarly, care must be taken on the descents with some very technical ground to be covered coming off Moel yr Ogof, but perhaps more so descending through Beddgelert Forest. The singletrack here never fails to excite, with fast-flowing switchbacks, rocky steps and a good amount of mud – you'll be grinning like a Cheshire cat at the bottom. Whether you'll run back up for a second lap may depend on how you found the climb of Moel Lefn!

As the time up high is fairly limited, the exposure time and risk of getting caught out are reduced. The clear ridgeline, some cairns and a fairly distinct trod from bwlch to bwlch makes navigation more simple, but this run should not be underestimated. Dropping off the western side would leave you in Cwm Pennant with no other way back than by retracing your steps.

ALTITUDE PROFILE

655

Metres

0

0   Km   2   4   6   8

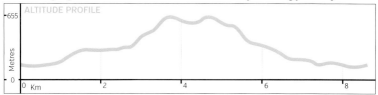

»» BEDDGELERT FOREST, MOEL LEFN & MOEL YR OGOF

DISTANCE 8.7KM »» ***ASCENT*** 558M »» ***TYPICAL TIME*** 1:30–2:30 HRS »» ***TERRAIN*** ROCKY/TECHNICAL »» ***NAVIGATION*** 3 – IN GOOD VISIBILITY ROUTE IS RELATIVELY EASY TO FOLLOW. IN POOR VISIBILITY TAKE CARE ASCENDING MOEL LEFN – ABILITY TO USE BEARINGS ESSENTIAL »» ***START/FINISH*** PONT CAE'R GORS CAR PARK, ACCESSED FROM THE MAIN ROAD AT SH 575509 »» ***GRID REF*** SH 574503 »» ***SATNAV*** LL54 6TN [NEAREST] »» ***OS MAP*** EXPLORER OL17 SNOWDON »» ***TRANSPORT*** BUSES STOP AT RHYD DDU FROM EITHER CAERNARFON OR PEN-Y-PASS »» ***REFRESHMENTS*** LOTS OF CAFES IN BEDDGELERT

DIRECTIONS >> BEDDGELERT FOREST, MOEL LEFN & MOEL YR OGOF

S **Turn right** out of the car park heading downhill. Follow the sign to *Beddgelert* crossing a bridge and the railway line then **bearing left** along a gravel fire road. Shortly you'll reach a T-junction and a house. Look **straight ahead** and go through the swing gate following the footpath up and **right** of the house into the forest. Once in the forest follow the yellow arrows on wooden posts. After climbing for 800m you'll reach a clearing: the path continues **straight ahead** but can be tricky to follow – try not to gain or lose any height and you'll know you're on the correct path as a rather flimsy-looking stile takes you back into the forest. Keep following the yellow arrows until you exit the forest for the second time.

2 Cross the stile and leave the forest, and turn 90 degrees to your **left**. Follow the fence, keeping it on your left, cross another stile and turn 90 degrees to your **right**. Follow the path with the small quarry on your left. The path climbs very steeply for what might seem like eternity.

3 As the angle starts to ease, the trod becomes a little harder to follow. If visibility is good follow the grassy trod up towards the rocky outcrop of Moel Lefn. However, if the visibility is poor, keep ascending; **at no point** should you start to descend before reaching the summit of Moel Lefn.

4 From the summit of Moel Lefn head south, descending rocky then grassy ground to reach a wall/fence with a large stile. Cross the stile and follow the broken rocky path to the summit of Moel yr Ogof. Descend steeply to reach a small pond with a wooden boardwalk over it. Continue through the rocky chasm and drop steeply to reach a broken wall. **Turn left** at the wall and follow a faint path with the wall on your right.

5 Carefully handrail the wall for 300m before crossing it and **turning right** down to the forest, a fence and a large wooden stile. The trusty yellow arrows are back; follow these once again. Descend quickly down the singletrack through the forest crossing several fire roads. After around 1.6km the path comes out on to a large, open fire road.

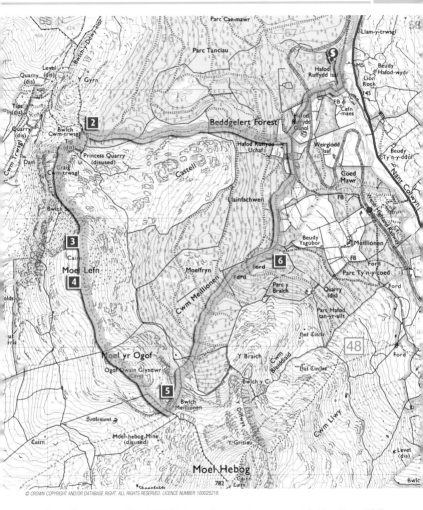

6   The yellow arrow will point right, towards a very large concrete bridge. **Do not** follow
the arrow but **turn left** instead. Pass a post with the number 17 on it and **bear right**.
Pass the yellow Forestry Commission barrier to reach the Hafod Ruffydd information
sign and not long after you'll arrive back at the T-junction and house which initially
lead into the forest. **Turn right** and retrace your steps back to the car park.

CAMERON CLIFF AND THOMAS BARTON ASCENDING YR EIFL » *PHOTO* JON BARTON

INTRODUCTION

Yr Eifl or The Rivals are the group of hills on the northern coast of the Llŷn Peninsula, an area of North Wales more often frequented by beach goers than mountain runners. As you drive south the hills are very distinct, their conical shapes and mountain-free backdrop accentuating their modest heights.

The Llŷn is often a good option on bad weather days as it seems to benefit from its own microclimate – the sun can be shining out here on even the wettest days in the mountains.

THE ROUTE

This route is a combination of singletrack trails, technical downhills, some tarmac and open bridleways. From the off you're heading up – the path is soon narrow, but runnable and never too steep. A breather on the summit is an absolute must – take a look around and you'll wonder why you've never been up here before. The descent off the summit is technical and care must be taken. It's short-lived but not worth risking an ankle. Once at the wall you can stretch your legs out again, dropping down to the road before turning back off to skirt around the northern slopes of the range. Varied trails bring you around to the Llŷn Coastal Path – turning on to this prepare yourself for a tough climb back over to the southern side of the range before cruising down to the car park along a wide and open 4x4 track.

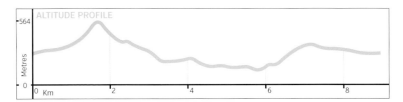

>> **TOUR OF YR EIFL**

DISTANCE 8.9KM >> **ASCENT** 384M >> **TYPICAL TIME** 1:20–2:00 HRS >> **TERRAIN** ROCKY/TECHNICAL >> **NAVIGATION** 3 - CARE NECESSARY IN POOR VISIBILITY, IT IS DIFFICULT TO FIND THE CORRECT PATH OFF YR EIFL >> **START/FINISH** YR EIFL CAR PARK NORTH OF LLITHFAEN >> **GRID REF** SH 352440 >> **SATNAV** LL53 6NU >> **OS MAP** EXPLORER 254 LLEYN PENINSULA EAST >> **REFRESHMENTS** CAFFI MEINIR, NANT GWRTHEYRN TEL: 01758 750 442

DIRECTIONS » TOUR OF YR EIFL

S From the car park head back along the road for 25m towards a path which runs alongside a wall. **Don't follow this**, but instead take the obvious and well-trodden path which heads off **left** at a 45-degree angle away from the wall. The path aims straight for the southern ridge of Yr Eifl. Continue on this path as it climbs steadily, cross an old, derelict wall and continue **straight ahead**. The path starts to narrow slightly but remains rutted and clear. As the path becomes increasingly steep take the **left fork** when the opportunity arises. You'll know you're nearing the summit as the path becomes more rocky.

2 From the summit, retrace your steps for 20m towards a smaller and very rocky summit to the east of the trig point. **Bear left** of this on the path, contouring for 100m before dropping steeply **down to runner's right** (east). Do your best to keep to this and join the wall. Continue down, crossing a fence. If you're feeling brave handrail the wall until you reach a metal swing gate; it is very, very rocky and difficult to run. The alternative is to bear to the right immediately after the fence to join an easier path – this is a little more difficult to find. If in doubt head back to the wall and keep with this until the gate.

3 Go through the gate and run **straight ahead**. At first the path is level but gradually increases in steepness as you drop down and **bear right**. Run past the obsolete A-frame stile and stick with this path until you reach the road. **Take care** going on to the road. **Turn left** and run for 300m until you reach a lay-by and gate. Go through the gate and head slightly **up and right**, across the field to another swing gate. Go through this and **bear slightly left** (if you reach *Private Land* turn left, uphill and keep the fence on your right). You'll reach another swing gate. After the gate follow the path dropping slightly downhill to another road.

4 Once on the road **turn left**. 100m after the antenna and just after dropping downhill there is a farm gate on your left; use the swing gate to the **left** and **turn right** keeping the wall on your right. For the next 1.5km keep the wall on your right – you'll go through a number of gates all in varying states of disrepair. Eventually you'll appear on a bizarre, alleyway-style path. **Turn left** on this and head very steeply uphill.

© CROWN COPYRIGHT AND/OR DATABASE RIGHT. ALL RIGHTS RESERVED. LICENCE NUMBER 100025218.

5 From here on follow the *Coastal Path* signs which will take you back to the start. Many will be relieved when cresting the top of the hill to be greeted with a path which resembles a motorway in comparison to the trods and snickets you've been navigating for the last 40 minutes. Enjoy the views down towards the Llŷn Peninsula as you cruise back down the hill. **Turn right** to the car park.

STEVE FRANKLIN APPROACHING THE STEEP BACK WALL OF CWM CAU

INTRODUCTION

Despite not being with the big three – Glyderau, Carneddau and Snowdon – the popularity of Cadair Idris is testament to the quality of the area and the mountain. Cwm Cau is a geographer's dream, the huge amphitheatre and steep back wall fall into Llyn Cau from which glacial moraine and deposits are aplenty. As you enter the cwm on the Minffordd Path the sense of grandeur is overwhelming. Despite the water temperature Llyn Cau makes a wonderful dip and is worth heading back up to once you've completed the horseshoe.

THE ROUTE

A spectacular run with fantastic positions. The route has two main climbs: the initial pull from the car park on the start of the Minffordd Path is tough – many of the sections are runnable but are interspersed with a few sets of steps. There's a moment's respite as you crest the edge of the cwm. For those with a real thirst for adventure there's an alternative route up the back wall of the cwm – it's steep and loose but exhilarating. The traditional option bears left up the steep but more solid path, rising to the horseshoe proper. From here the position is wonderful, perched on the edge with the plummet down to Llyn Cau on the right and views out to Harlech and the Llŷn Peninsula on the left.

From the summit the running is easier and not quite as exposed. Grassy paths lead to the summit of Mynydd Moel before a steep and technical path descends to rejoin the Minffordd Path. The steep start is much better in reverse – if you've still some spring left then you can bound your way back down to the car park in double time!

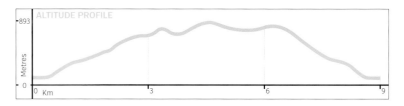

ALTITUDE PROFILE

>> CADAIR IDRIS

DISTANCE 9KM >> *ASCENT* 981M >> *TYPICAL TIME* 2:00-4:00 HRS >> *TERRAIN* ROCKY/TECHNICAL, OPEN FELL OR HANDS ON >> *NAVIGATION* 3 – THE ROUTE IS QUITE EASY TO FOLLOW IN GOOD VISIBILITY BUT REMEMBER THIS IS A BIG MOUNTAIN, THE WEATHER WILL BE DIFFERENT UP HIGH TO IN THE CAR PARK AND THE REPERCUSSIONS OF AN ERROR ARE SERIOUS >> *START/FINISH* DÔL IDRIS PAY & DISPLAY CAR PARK AT MINFFORDD >> *GRID REF* SH 732115 >> *SATNAV* LL36 9AJ >> *OS MAP* EXPLORER OL23 CADAIR IDRIS & LLYN TEGID >> *REFRESHMENTS* TŶ TE CADAIR TEA ROOM TEL: 01654 761 505; TOILETS IN CAR PARK

DIRECTIONS » CADAIR IDRIS

S From the car park head through the swing gate and follow signs to the *Cafe* and *Cadair Idris*. Pass the cafe and take the steep path through the gate on the **right**. Climb steeply for some time with the river to your right. The path changes between stones steps and gravel but remains steep. At the large slate bridge follow the signpost to Llyn Cau. The path remains good and a little less steep. As you breach the lip of the cwm look for the slanted rock slabs to your right: the optional route starts from here.

2 The 'normal' route up is no walk in the park. From the slanting slabs **turn left** following the clear, stepped path steeply uphill. At the top of this climb take a **right** at the cairn along the ridgeline, shortly passing another cairn. Carry on along the ridge, taking care not to stray too close to the edge – it's a big drop! Continue along this path as it starts to climb again up loose rocky terrain, and cross an A-frame stile to reach the summit of Craig Cwm Amarch. Drop off this down some technical singletrack to reach the bwlch between Craig Cwm Amarch and Cadair Idris.

OPTIONAL ROUTE

OR If you're feeling adventurous go straight ahead past the slabs to reach Llyn Cau. Circumnavigate the llyn with it on your left, crossing a river. Once you reach the opposite side of the llyn look steeply up and **take care** while you scramble your way up the steep back wall of Cwm Cau. Remember to take care; it is loose and steep. Also, remember there may be walkers above you either on your path or walking the ridgeline so keep an eye out above. Once you reach the bwlch between Craig Cwm Amarch and Cadair Idris **turn right**.

3 From the bwlch, keep on the main path climbing steeply; the path wiggles a little but is clear to follow with regular cairns along the route. As you near the summit of Cadair the terrain becomes increasingly rocky until you reach the trig point. There is a great bothy shelter on the summit to escape the elements if they aren't behaving.

Directions continue overleaf

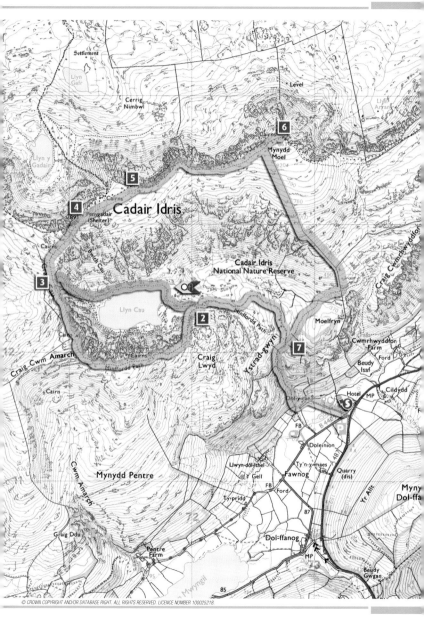

Cadair Idris

Cadair Idris
National Nature Reserve

DIRECTIONS >> CADAIR IDRIS

4   **Take care** to find the correct path off Cadair. If the visibility is good then it's not tricky, but should the summit be in the cloud it's more problematic. The path is not clear for the first 50m but it soon turns into a very obvious 1m-wide rocky track. A bearing of 80° should get you to the path. An alternative method is to stand with your back to the bothy shelter beneath the old roof beam protruding from the wall: the beam points directly towards the path you need to follow.

5   The running from here towards Mynydd Moel is fantastic, a combination of spongy grass and trails. There aren't many features to look out for on this stretch; the path undulates but is never too steep, **ensure** you don't drop steeply to your right. **Do not** take the path downhill to your right but climb gradually to the summit of Mynydd Moel.

6   50m before the summit cross the A-frame stile, grab the summit, retrace your steps over the stile and **turn left** downhill while keeping the fence to your left. Descend for some time, crossing the fence on your **left** at the second stile (not including the stile at the top). Remain on the recently renovated path to cross another stile on your **right**. The path continues to descend but a little less steeply.

7   Cross the large slate bridge and **turn left** downhill retracing your initial steps to the cafe and then car park.

MOUNTAIN RUNNING BY LLYN CAU

STEVE FRANKLIN RETURNING FROM THE MOELWYNS LOOP

10 >> MOELWYN BACH & MOELWYN MAWR   9.2km

INTRODUCTION

Another hidden gem. The southern Moelwyns afford unique views of Snowdonia and the coast to the south. Surprisingly, the view from the smaller of the two – Moelwyn Bach – offers a more encompassing view of the area, giving a magnificent panorama of the coastline, Moelwyns, Snowdon and Moel Hebog. The old quarry buildings, inclines and slate structures are well worth exploring. It's hard to grasp the size and scale of some of the buildings that once stood here, as well as the enormous manpower that must have been required to run the mining operations.

THE ROUTE

This is a fine introduction to fell running. The gentle start up the access road to Llyn Stwlan reservoir is great way to get the legs going and take in the spectacular views to the south. The juxtaposition of the disused Trawsfynydd nuclear power station (the large and distinctly out-of-place building on the horizon) and the surrounding area is oddly mesmerising and boggles the mind as to how they were ever allowed to build it.

Both the Moelwyns on this run are wonderful hills. They pack a punch for their relatively small size and at times require some hands-on-knees walking.

ALTITUDE PROFILE

Metres | 770 ... 0

0 Km · 3 · 6 · 9

>> MOELWYN BACH & MOELWYN MAWR

DISTANCE 9.2KM >> **ASCENT** 506M >> **TYPICAL TIME** 1:15–2:30 HRS >> **TERRAIN** PATHS/TRODS, ROCKY/ TECHNICAL, OPEN FELL OR HANDS ON >> **NAVIGATION** 3 – NECESSARY IN POOR VISIBILITY. BEARING REQUIRED TO SAFELY GET OFF MOELWYN MAWR >> **START/FINISH** LAY-BY AT HEAD OF CWMORTHIN ROAD ABOVE TANYGRISIAU >> **GRID REF** SH 683454 >> **SATNAV** LL41 3ST >> **OS MAP** EXPLORER OL17 SNOWDON; EXPLORER OL18 HARLECH, PORTHMADOG & BALA >> **REFRESHMENTS** LAKESIDE CAFE, TANYGRISIAU TEL: 01766 830 950

DIRECTIONS » MOELWYN BACH & MOELWYN MAWR

S From the car park go through the **left-hand gate** immediately crossing a large footbridge. Continue on the obvious path until you reach a single-track road. Follow this road for 1.5km. Look out for a footpath sign on your **left** and a bridge made of railway sleepers. Cross this and the stile and **turn right** keeping the fence on your right until you're 50m from the dam wall. Take a **sharp left** up a steep gully. At the top of the gully, keeping the dam wall on your right, aim for the leftmost corner of the dam.

2 From the leftmost corner of the dam stay on the very boggy path just south of the llyn. **Do not** take the path heading south no matter how dry it looks! The boggy path leads to a cairn in the bwlch between the two Moelwyns. **Turn left** to Moelwyn Bach. **Be careful**, do not take the obvious, walled, wide path but instead start to head immediately uphill and within 25m you'll join a well-trodden, rutted path. Keep on this all the way to the summit. Take a look over your right shoulder as you approach the summit and check out Moelwyn Mawr; some may regret the decision to go up Moelwyn Bach. To descend, **retrace your steps** back to the cairn in the bwlch.

3 Follow the only path up on to the southern ridge of Moelwyn Mawr; it is narrow but well-used and easy to stick to. Keep on this until you reach the trig point. (How many false summits did you count?)

4 Descending off Moelwyn Mawr is the trickiest part of the loop, especially in poor visibility. **If visibility is poor, follow a compass bearing from the trig point of 92° for 60m.** At this point the path becomes very clear and is narrow but deeply rutted. Keep on this path – it runs parallel with a fence. Cross the fence at the third stile with an old, stone building to your right. Continue **straight ahead**, gradually **bearing left** to run alongside a long mound of slate until you reach the top of a slate incline.

5 Drop steeply down the incline and head into the quarry proper. Run through the old station house and head for the main path and slate finger-stone, **straight ahead**. Navigation is easy from now on. Keep on this path, passing Llyn Cwmorthin. Cross the bridge at the llyn's southern tip and go downhill on the wide shale path back to the car park.

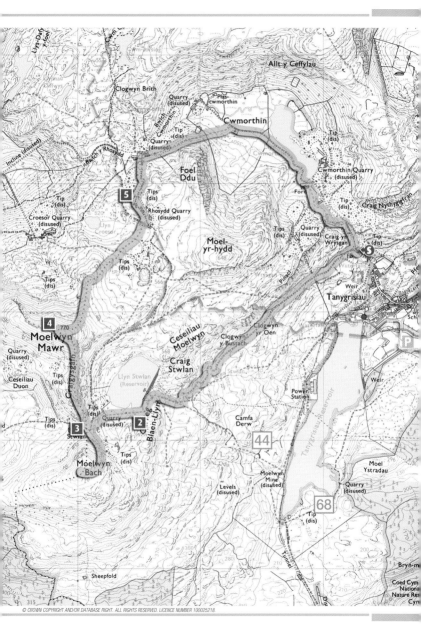

SARAH CHRISTIAN ON THE OLD DAM WALL BY LLYN DULYN » *PHOTO* STEVE FRANKLIN

11 » EASTERN CARNEDDAU: LLYN DULYN

9.5km

INTRODUCTION

Llyn Dulyn (the Black Lake) and Melyn-llyn lie high above the Conwy valley. Both lakes are dark, foreboding and steeped in history. Llyn Dulyn was known as the 'airplane graveyard' during WWII as it was a magnet for doomed aircraft – over a dozen planes crashed into the lake and at very low water levels it's possible to see the propellers from one of these unfortunate incidents.

THE ROUTE

This is a mini adventure into the remote Cwm Dulyn, and is without lots of hills. Perched on the eastern flanks of the Carneddau the cwm can't be seen from the parking at Cwm Eigiau, a valley which attracts much more attention, and is not easily accessed from anywhere else, although many will have walked/run above the cwm while taking on the Welsh 3,000ers. As you make your way up the valley towards Melynllyn and Dulyn there is a rather dark and ominous feel. The huge east-facing steep back walls block out much of the daylight and plummet straight into the eerie black water.

Cwm Dulyn is accessed via a steady climb over Clogwynyreryr on to the Maldy path. The path is easy to follow, climbing gently for one kilometre before descending down to the first of the two llyns. A wonderfully technical downhill section links the lakes and drops you at the Dulyn dam. From here the downhill path picks its way through the boulder-strewn hillside, passing through one of the earliest-known roundhouse settlements in Britain. Alas the dry paths can't last forever and the going gets a bit boggy, but at least it's downhill towards the dam where the Dulyn valley opens out. All that's left is a pleasant contour around Cerrig Cochion before retracing your steps to the parking at Cwm Eigiau.

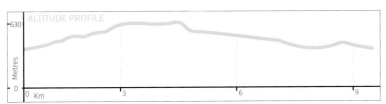

ALTITUDE PROFILE

630 | Metres | 0

0 Km · · · 3 · · · 6 · · · 9

» EASTERN CARNEDDAU: LLYN DULYN

DISTANCE 9.5KM » *ASCENT* 250M » *TYPICAL TIME* 0:50–1:30 HRS » *TERRAIN* PATHS/TRODS » *NAVIGATION* 2 – GENERALLY EASY THOUGH CARE SHOULD BE TAKEN FINDING PATH TO CERRIG COCHION DAM » *START/FINISH* LAY-BY NEAR LLYN EIGIAU » *GRID REF* SH 732663 » *SATNAV* LL32 8SH [NEAREST] » *OS MAP* EXPLORER OL17 SNOWDON » *REFRESHMENTS* NONE AT PARKING. LOTS OF CAFES IN THE CONWY VALLEY

DIRECTIONS >> EASTERN CARNEDDAU: LLYN DULYN

S   From the Llyn Eigiau car parking (space for ten cars) cross the stile and take the paved track north-west running at a 90° angle to the road. After 600m cross another stile going **straight ahead** between two very large boulders. Follow the track around to the left and then back right, gradually gaining height. Keep on it around the sharp left-hand corner to reach a gate and A-frame stile. Cross the stile and go **straight ahead**. Continue past a large finger-stone and small dogleg in the path before reaching a metal gate and wooden stile.

2   Keep on the Clogwyn Maldy track for 2km, climbing initially before descending gently down to a bridge and the ruins of an old mill. Cross the bridge following the track uphill to reach the tip of Melynllyn. Cross the river with care bearing **rightwards** down the steep and rocky path. This is the most technical section of the run but is relatively short-lived. At the old dam wall drop down and **right** on a narrow but well-trodden path running beneath the dam wall. Find a suitable place to cross the river on to the grassy plateau.

3   Head eastwards, just below the boulder field, towards the large, patchwork hut. The path runs 30m above the hut and can be difficult to follow as you're paying more attention to where you're putting your feet! As the boulder field ends the path becomes wetter and there is the temptation to lose height. Pass a few hundred metres above the copse of trees which should be down and to your right. Cross the metal stile and continue **straight ahead** contouring along and keeping your height. Shortly after crossing a second metal stile cross the river at the bridge (or another suitable point should you have dropped too low) and take the path downhill to your **right** until you reach the dam wall.

4   Cross the stile on to and over the dam wall and **turn left** on the other side towards the wide track. Once on the track follow it as it contours around to the **right** for 800m. This brings you out at the two large boulders you passed between at the start of the run. **Turn left** here, over the stile and keep on the wide track back to the car park.

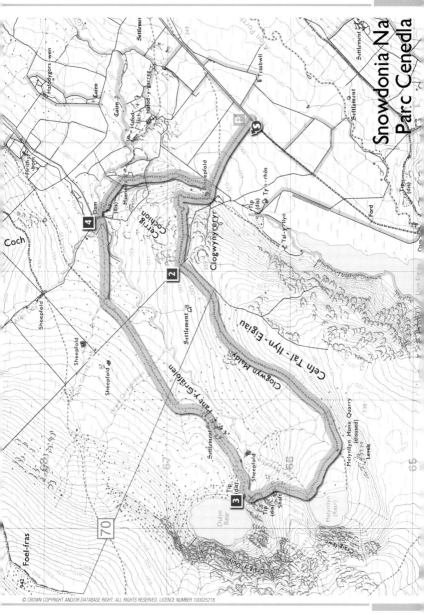

Snowdonia Na
Parc Cenedla

Coch

Foel-fras

© CROWN COPYRIGHT AND/OR DATABASE RIGHT. ALL RIGHTS RESERVED. LICENCE NUMBER 100025218.

HEADING BACK INTO CROESOR, WITH CNICHT DOMINATING THE SKYLINE

INTRODUCTION

The Croesor valley lies at the southern end of the Moelwyns and is overlooked by Cnicht to the north. Cnicht is not actually classed as a stand-alone mountain as it is not considered to be distinct enough from its neighbour Allt-fawr, despite the latter being over four kilometres away. However, Cnicht most certainly looks and feels like a mountain, so much so that it is informally known as the 'Matterhorn of Wales', a result of its striking shape when viewed from the south-west.

This is a route requiring a plethora of mountain-running skills, but one skill you won't need is the ability to dodge people.

THE ROUTE

A testing run in one of the most spectacular valleys in North Wales, and best enjoyed in the evening light. The route has a tough start, heading directly up Cnicht, but the position along the ridge is worth every ounce of effort. Both the descent off the summit and the singletrack path back down towards Croesor are just brilliant, testing but never too difficult. Perhaps the best thing about this run is how quiet the area is in comparison to the more major mountains in Snowdonia.

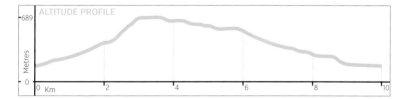

>> CROESOR & CNICHT

DISTANCE 10KM ›› *ASCENT* 425M ›› *TYPICAL TIME* 1:30–3:00 HRS ›› *TERRAIN* ROCKY/TECHNICAL, OPEN FELL OR HANDS ON ›› *NAVIGATION* 3 – SOME NAVIGATION MAY BE NEEDED TO CROSS THE FLATS BY THE LLYNS. IN POOR VISIBILITY THE LANDSCAPE IS QUITE DISORIENTATING & THE ABILITY TO USE A BEARING IS IMPORTANT. IN GOOD VISIBILITY THE NAVIGATION IS VERY EASY ›› *START/FINISH* CAR PARK IN CROESOR ›› *GRID REF* SH 631446 ›› *SATNAV* LL48 6SR ›› *OS MAP* EXPLORER OL17 SNOWDON; EXPLORER OL18 HARLECH, PORTHMADOG & BALA ›› *REFRESHMENTS* ORIEL CAFFI CROESOR (SEASONAL) TEL: 01766 771 433; PUBLIC TOILET IN CAR PARK

S   Exit the car park and **turn right** on to the road, following the large signpost marked *Cnicht*. Run on the road, climbing steeply. Pass through a metal swing gate on to a path. Go **straight ahead**, gaining height quickly. As the path levels go through the large wooden gate on the **right**.

2   Continue along the path, passing over a large wooden stile. Shortly after the stile follow the signpost pointing **right**, over a stile and on to the ridge proper. Ascend gradually towards an outcrop, cross another stile on to a rocky path and **turn right** almost immediately. From here on, stick to the singletrack path, never really leaving the ridgeline.

3   From the first, false, summit, continue **straight ahead** along the ridge and over the true summit. The path remains well trodden but narrows in width. Descend gradually along a blunt ridge; **try not to stray off left**. As you draw almost level with Llyn yr Adar (on your left) a large cairn appears.

4   **Turn right** – the paths drops quickly before levelling off. There is a path which weaves between Llyn Cwm-corsiog and Llynnau Diffwys, however it's not always easy to stick to. Thankfully the path leading out of the quarries down towards the Croesor valley is impossible to pass without realising. Once you hit the path **turn right**, towards Croesor. As you approach the head of the valley look for the large wooden post, signposting *Croesor*.

5   **Turn left** off the main track and follow the smaller path down towards a river. It's rocky at first but soon smoothens out and is wonderful fun to run. Stay on this path, passing old inclines, gates and stiles until you reach a large wooden stile next to a metal gate. Cross the stile and drop down to the road by the house. **Turn left.** After the second cattle grid, **turn right** just after the house, go through two gates and **turn left**. Continue alongside the river until at the car park; cross at the large wooden bridge.

GLYN HUDSON AND BECKY LOUNDS ON THE NEW PATH BY LLYN DINAS

13 ≫ LLYN DINAS

10.3km

INTRODUCTION

The Nant Gwynant valley separates the Snowdon range from the Moelwyns. This route explores many historical landmarks, some much older than others, and makes for a low-level run on a wide variety of terrain. The visit to Dinas Emrys is not to be missed!

THE ROUTE

The initial section of the Watkin Path is strewn with remnants from the mining industry, but it is Dinas Emrys which has the most interesting history. Not much remains of the Iron Age hill fort which stood on the site back in the first century. However, the legend of King Arthur has it that Dinas Emrys was the site of the famous exchange between Vortigern and Merlin, where Merlin explained Vortigern's hill fort could not stand here due to

the hidden pool containing the white (Saxon) and red (Welsh) dragons!

As the route stays low in the valley it's a good option in bad weather, navigation is straightforward and the terrain is a combination of natural and man-made footpaths. The ascent is limited to the first few kilometres of the run, making it a great option if your legs are a little tired.

The latter part of the run takes you along the shores of Llyn Dinas. The llyn is a mere ten metres deep, meaning, unlike a number of the other llyns, it warms up quickly and so is a wonderful spot for refreshing your legs post run. Another delight of the route is Caffi Gwynant, a splendid cafe at the start of the route. Their lunches, cakes and coffee are some of the best in North Wales!

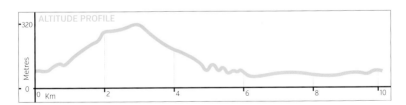

ALTITUDE PROFILE

≫ LLYN DINAS

DISTANCE 10.3KM ≫ **ASCENT** 185M ≫ **TYPICAL TIME** 1:00-2:00 HRS ≫ **TERRAIN** PATHS/TRODS ≫ **NAVIGATION** 3 - GENERALLY EASY ON GOOD, CLEAR PATHS. TAKE CARE AFTER LEAVING THE WATKIN PATH BENEATH BYLCHAU TERFYN AS THIS CAN BE DIFFICULT IN POOR VISIBILITY ≫ **START/FINISH** LAY-BY SOUTH OF CAFFI GWYNANT OR CAR PARK AT START OF WATKIN PATH (SH 628507) ≫ **GRID REF** SH 627506 ≫ **SATNAV** LL55 4NL ≫ **OS MAP** EXPLORER OL17 SNOWDON ≫ **TRANSPORT** BUSES BETWEEN BEDDGELERT AND PEN-Y-PASS ≫ **REFRESHMENTS** CAFFI GWYNANT TEL: 01766 890 855; MORE CAFES AND ICE CREAM IN BEDDGELERT; PUBLIC TOILETS AT START OF WATKIN PATH

S From the car park, follow the Watkin Path (depending on the time of year you may be sharing the first 1.5km with a number of tourists) initially through the woods, breaking out as the river becomes visible straight ahead. The path trends left away from the river and starts to climb. As it bears back towards the river, cross the disused incline and take the path on the **left** signposted *Craflwyn*.

2 Contour underneath the large bank on your right, staying downhill of the wall. There are regular wooden posts with black arrows on to help direct you. After crossing the second ladder stile, **drop down and left** past the old quarry buildings.

3 **Continue downhill** on the large path to the river proper where there is a large wooden bridge and an old building to your right. **Continue straight ahead** (do not cross the river). The track descends quickly; either follow it around the dogleg or cut the corner off by dropping down the steep grassy bank towards a large drystone wall. **Turn right** at the wall, following it until you reach the stile and signpost to *Glastir*.

4 Follow the track out and back to Dinas Emrys. **You must retrace your steps** as there is no other way off Dinas Emrys. From the stile, follow the wall until you reach the main path, and cross a large stone bridge passing the crystal-clear fairy pool. Continue along the path until you're able to see a yellow house. Take the footpath to the **left** of the house and head down towards the main road.

5 **Cross the road** and join the footpath immediately opposite. **Head left**, with the river on your right. At the Sygun Copper Mine, cross the river and take the path on the **left**. Follow the Afon Glaslyn river towards Llyn Dinas. As you reach Llyn Dinas **do not** cross the bridge but instead **trend right** along the southern flank. There is a newly laid path (not on the OS map) along the shore of the llyn. At the end of the llyn go through Llyndy Isaf Farm and **turn left** at the road. Cross the bridge and continue north along the A498 (carefully) for a few hundred metres back to the start.

INTRODUCTION

Alwen Reservoir and nearby Llyn Brenig are great locations for family days out. Easy-going trails in a beautiful location and quite probably in an area of Wales you've never been to before. Alwen Reservoir is not only great for running but also has numerous mountain bike trails, fishing, horse riding and water sports nearby. It is surrounded by both moorland and forest, which makes for a diverse ecosystem – keep your eyes peeled for red squirrels, black grouse and large heath butterflies.

THE ROUTE

This run is entirely on footpaths and starts by crossing the rather imposing, early twentieth-century dam wall. Upon entering the woodland on the western flank, an undulating path leads out on to open moorland before crossing the northern tip on the 130-metre-long footbridge. A short climb leads back into the woodland, only this time it feels like something out of *Lord of the Rings* as the path twists and turns through the dense forest before reaching the reservoir shore and returning to the dam.

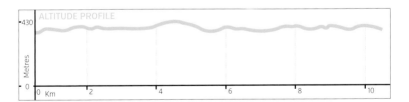

>> ALWEN RESERVOIR

DISTANCE 10.6KM ≫ **ASCENT** 95M ≫ **TYPICAL TIME** 1:00–1:30 HRS ≫ **TERRAIN** ROAD/FIRE ROAD, TRAIL ≫ **NAVIGATION** 1 – EASILY NAVIGABLE IN ALL WEATHER, SIGNPOSTED AND CLEAR TRACKS ≫ **START/FINISH** CAR PARK BY DAM WALL AT SOUTHERN END OF ALWEN RESERVOIR ≫ **GRID REF** SH 956529 ≫ **SATNAV** LL21 9TT ≫ **OS MAP** EXPLORER 264 VALE OF CLWYD ≫ **REFRESHMENTS** CAFE, INFORMATION CENTRE AND TOILETS AT NEARBY LLYN BRENIG TEL: 01490 420 463

S Head out over the Alwen dam wall, **turning right** immediately after and tracing the edge of the reservoir – follow the Alwen Trail light blue waymarkers. Continue through the forest on wide and curving fire roads. The path undulates but is never continuously steep. As you break out of the forest climb gradually on the singletrack path, leading to open ground and some fantastic views.

2 On the crest of the hill at the gate continue **straight ahead**. (It is possible to venture off left to the summit of Mwdwl-eithin following the fence line from the gate. This is much more difficult than the rest of the route – if you do do this, retrace your steps back along the fence line to the gate.) From the gate, open up your stride and roll down to the large, wooden bridge crossing the northern tip of the reservoir.

3 Cross the bridge and continue **straight ahead** towards the large stone house. **Turn right** before the house, re-entering the forest. Weave your way through the woods and down to the reservoir shore. Cross the tributary via the newly built bridge and not the older bridge nearer to the water's edge.

4 After crossing the bridge, follow the paths, which widen out into fire roads, down to the water's edge. Continue on the fire roads, never trending too far from the water, weaving in and out of the woodland. As the track opens up **keep right**, passing a building firstly on your right and another shortly after on your left. As you near the dam wall be sure to take the **right fork**, leading back to the car park.

EMMA TRUMAN AND MARK TAYLOR ON THE CLIMB UP THE MAESGWM VALLEY

11.6km

INTRODUCTION

Moel Eilio and its sister peaks Foel Gron and Foel Goch command the skyline above Llanberis. They aren't the most dominant summits, but their continuous string and rolling shapes just ask to be run over, making for a great route with breathtaking views of the Glyders, Snowdon and the Nantlle Ridge. Runs are often referred to as 'classics' – but this loop really is!

THE ROUTE

The route starts off kindly, gently cruising the length of the summits on the flat. Count them as you go and mentally tick them off as you summit each one later in the run. The climb up Maesgwm valley is gradual at first on a good path. However, just before reaching the bwlch at the trail head the path rears up and gives you a taste of what's to come. A final little push gets you to the bwlch and it's worth stopping, whether you need to or not,

to take in the breathtaking views of Nant y Betws, framed by the climbs on either side of you, and – straight ahead – the Nantlle Ridge, one of the best linear routes to run or walk in Snowdonia.

It's from the bwlch that the meat of the route begins and the start of the ridge-running proper. Each climb is steep, but thankfully never too long, and is followed by brilliant descending. Once at the summit of Moel Eilio be sure to look back at where you've come; Snowdon dominates the skyline, splitting the two valleys.

The descent off Eilio is wonderful; soft and bouncy grass runs the entire length of the ridge, the perfect angle to reach terminal running velocity without feeling out of control. As the gradient eases bear right back towards Llanberis, dropping steeply down fields and passing several wonderful old iron gates.

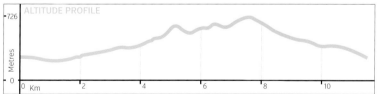

ALTITUDE PROFILE

≫ MOEL EILIO

DISTANCE 11.6KM ≫ *ASCENT* 660M ≫ *TYPICAL TIME* 1:30–3:00 HRS ≫ *TERRAIN* PATHS/TRODS ≫ *NAVIGATION* 2 – ROUTEFINDING IS GENERALLY EASY AND REGULAR FENCES AND STILES HELP TO MARK THE WAY. THE MOUNTAINS GET THE BRUNT OF THE WEATHER SO CARRYING SPARE KIT IS ALWAYS A GOOD IDEA ≫ *START/FINISH* LAY-BY AT FRON GOCH ROAD HEAD, 1.5KM SOUTH-WEST OF LLANBERIS ≫ *GRID REF* SH 569597 ≫ *SATNAV* LLANBERIS ≫ *OS MAP* EXPLORER OL17 SNOWDON ≫ *TRANSPORT* BUS TO LLANBERIS FROM BANGOR ≫ *REFRESHMENTS* CAFES, SHOPS AND TOILETS ARE ALL AVAILABLE IN LLANBERIS

S *Finding the start is perhaps more difficult than navigating the route! Turn off Llanberis high street towards the YHA. Turn right again on to Fron Goch and then left towards Plas Garnedd Care Centre. Continue up the narrow single-track road, going through a gate (remember to shut it after you've been through), and keep going until you reach the road head and parking for three cars.*

From the parking drop back down the road for 20m and **turn right** along the bridleway. Cross the highly (overly) engineered bridge and continue **straight ahead**. Remain on the bridleway passing through several gates. As the bridleway turns to tarmac go **straight ahead**. **Bear right** following the road/track to cross another bridge and go through a large gate.

2 Climb gently up the good path, passing through another gate just before a small cottage on your left. The path gains height, gradually heading towards Bwlch Maesgwm. Just before the bwlch the path steepens; a sign of things to come.

3 At the bwlch, **do not** cross any stiles or go through any gates. **Turn right**, keeping the fence to your left, and aim for the lone boulder located halfway up the slope. The path is steep but well trodden and easy to follow to the summit of Foel Goch. At the summit, cross the stile, with the fence to your left, and follow the path descending down the soft, bouncy grass to another plateau. Continue **straight ahead**, passing an old iron fence post on your way up Foel Gron. As you near the top of Foel Gron the path peters out slightly; **bear gently right** for about 20m, the path will become prominent again as it zigzags back left and steeply down for a short distance before gradually gaining height again.

4 Cross the stile and descend to Bwlch Cwm Cesig. Set off up Moel Eilio, with the fence to your right: the million-dollar question is do you run or walk? It's steep but not for too long. Shortly before the summit go over the stile and stone wall. The best line to the summit is to handrail the fence to your left. Follow this to the shelter and cairn.

5   On leaving the shelter **bear left**. Keep the fence line to your left but do not cross it. Hop over the boggy patch and stepping stones and begin to descend with increasing velocity. Keep the fence on your left, until it cuts sharply left and the path continues straight ahead. **Follow the path.** The ground becomes less steep as you near the old quarries. At the gate and wall junction **turn right** on to the byway and **do not** cross any boundaries. Keep on the byway, passing through two old metal swing gates. After the second gate the path steepens before reaching a road. Continue for another few hundred metres to reach the parking area.

TONY AND SARAH WHITEHOUSE RETURNING ON THE NANT Y BENGLOG BYWAY

14km

INTRODUCTION

A tough run and good introduction to fell running. It follows paths throughout but they aren't always easy to keep to and are interspersed with some rather soggy patches. This really is a demanding one and will be an excellent run to strengthen the legs over some rough terrain. If you're up for a challenge, give it a go.

THE ROUTE

The climbing starts almost immediately out of Capel up towards Gallt yr Ogof. Should you need a rest on the climb be sure to look up and take in the majesty of the Snowdon Horseshoe to the south-west. Once up high there's some steady running towards the Glyders, with the iconic summit of Tryfan to your right.

The descent down Cwm Tryfan will test the best; it starts off steep and loose and turns into some very technical singletrack. This descent combined with the earlier ascent make this a great route if you're up for a testing run.

For those with anything left in their pins, the valley path down Nant y Benglog is very quick in comparison with the rest of the route. Those who left their legs behind will find the views of the Carneddau are pleasantly distracting.

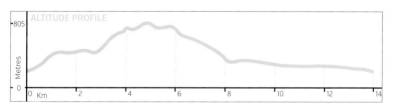

ALTITUDE PROFILE

805

Metres

0

0 Km   2   4   6   8   10   12   14

≫ Y FOEL GOCH & CWM TRYFAN

DISTANCE 14KM ≫ **ASCENT** 575M ≫ **TYPICAL TIME** 1:30–2:30 HRS ≫ **TERRAIN** ROCKY/TECHNICAL, OPEN FELL OR HANDS ON ≫ **NAVIGATION** 5 – IN POOR VISIBILITY COMPASS SKILLS ARE VITAL. THE PATH LEADING UP FROM CAPEL CURIG TOWARDS GALLT YR OGOF IS NOT ALWAYS OBVIOUS AND NOT CONTINUOUS, SOME MOUNTAIN SENSE IS KEY TO KEEP ON IT ≫ **START/FINISH** PAY & DISPLAY CAR PARK BEHIND JOE BROWNS SHOP IN CAPEL CURIG ≫ **GRID REF** SH 720582 ≫ **SATNAV** LL24 0EN ≫ **OS MAP** EXPLORER OL17 SNOWDON ≫ **TRANSPORT** REGULAR BUSES FROM BETHESDA, BETWS-Y-COED, LLANBERIS AND BEDDEGELERT ≫ **REFRESHMENTS** CAFE, VILLAGE SHOP, PUBLIC TOILETS & JOE BROWNS OUTDOOR SHOP IN CAPEL CURIG

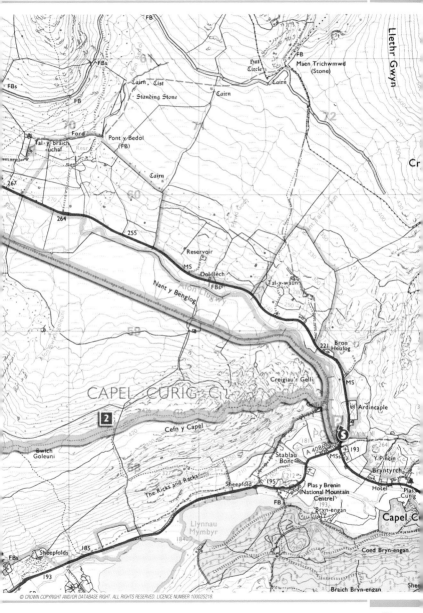

S   From the car park head north across the cattle grid and up the farm drive to reach a gate and stile. Cross the stile and **turn left**. Follow the fence for 10m and as it bears left go **straight ahead** into the reeds ... a path appears! The path weaves its way up the hillside; at times it splits but always comes back to a main path. **If in doubt** at any point keep to runner's right of the ridgeline and main bank of rocks. Once over the first summit of Cefn y Capel a brief descent leads down to a plateau and some wet ground. Climb briefly before reaching a fence line and wooden stile.

2   Cross the stile, climb briefly and descend again before crossing another boggy plateau. The ground starts to steepen and an old wall line is joined. Follow the wall on its left, crossing another wall via a wooden stile. With a fence line on your right and old wall to the left climb very steeply until the path meets the fence.

3   Handrail the fence for a very short distance and, as the fence line bears right and uphill (towards Gallt yr Ogof), take the path **straight ahead**, contouring around Gallt yr Ogof before climbing again to reach the bwlch between Gallt yr Ogof and Y Foel Goch. Pass a small pond (there is a path either side of it, both are boggy!) and climb for one last time up on to Y Foel Goch. Pass to the **right** of the cairn/shelter on the summit and take the obvious path down to Llyn Caseg-fraith. The llyn is obvious in good visibility. After passing the llyn on its left continue until you reach the large cairn marking the junction with the Miner's Track.

4   **Turn right**, downhill, into Cwm Tryfan. It's very steep at first and quite loose so take care. After the initial steepness it levels but maintains interest by being very rocky (and much more difficult in the wet). The path is very clear and easy to follow down to Gwern Gof Uchaf campsite.

5   At the campsite, **bear right** along the byway track, soon crossing a bridge. Continue along the byway passing through Gwern Gof Isaf campsite. Keep on this track for another 4km back to Capel Curig – there are no other paths to take before arriving back at the car park.

LOOKING ACROSS CWM TRYFAN TO TRYFAN

BECKY LOUNDS CLIMBING THE RANGER PATH

17 » SNOWDON: RHYD DDU & THE RANGER PATH

14.1km

INTRODUCTION

An adventure to the summit of Snowdon via one of the lesser-travelled routes. While the southern flanks of the mountain appear gentler than the northern, don't be fooled into thinking this is a gentle route, or one to be underestimated. Mountain sense is vital for this run, particularly when – as is often the case – the upper slopes are shrouded in cloud.

THE ROUTE

After a steady start up through the disused quarries, the slate trails make way for the Ranger Path. The Ranger Path rises above Llyn Ffynnon-y-gwas to the foot of the shoulder of Clogwyn Du'r Arddu and it's here that the proper climbing begins. Head up, taking switchback after switchback, slowly but steadily gaining height. As the switchbacks trend left take

a look into the distance at the ants summiting Snowdon via the popular Llanberis Path. As the path straightens the angle relents, bearing right to cross the Snowdon Railway, passing the fingerstone which marks the junction with the Pyg Track. From here to the summit you're likely to be sharing the paths. The summit can be crowded on weekends and sunny days but if you take a minute to look you'll find some solace. The descent is technical at first, running the ridgeline south. The path weaves its way along the ridge, nipping from side to side. The path opens out and swings right, running the crest of the Cwm Clogwyn horseshoe. It's from here that the paths ease in their angle and the running becomes easier, following the well-marked and trodden paths back towards Rhyd Ddu.

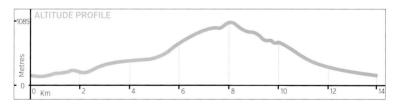

ALTITUDE PROFILE

1085

Metres

0

0 Km   2   4   6   8   10   12   14

» SNOWDON: RHYD DDU & THE RANGER PATH

DISTANCE 14.1KM » **ASCENT** 970M » **TYPICAL TIME** 2:00–5:00 HRS » **TERRAIN** ROCKY/TECHNICAL » **NAVIGATION 3** - NOT THE TRICKIEST BUT AN ERROR COULD BE COSTLY, BOTH IN TERMS OF ENDING UP A LONG WAY FROM THE CAR OR BY DROPPING OVER A LARGE PRECIPICE! » **START/FINISH** PAY & DISPLAY CAR PARK IN RHYD DDU » **GRID REF** SH 571525 » **SATNAV** LL54 6TN » **OS MAP** EXPLORER OL17 SNOWDON » **TRANSPORT** BUSES FROM CAENARFON AND BEDDGELERT » **REFRESHMENTS** EXCELLENT PUB IN RHYD DDU – CWELLYN ARMS TEL: 01766 890 321; PUBLIC TOILETS IN THE CAR PARK

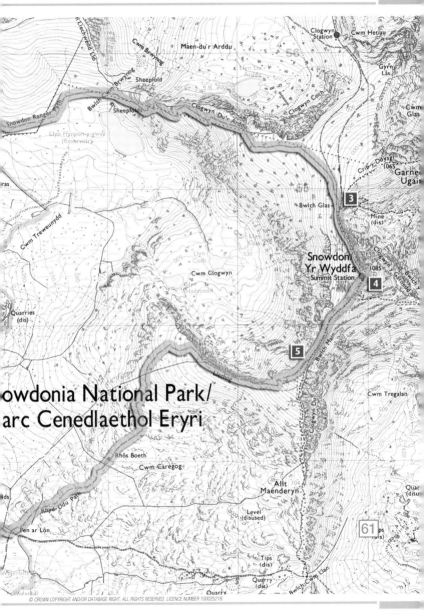

DIRECTIONS >> SNOWDON: RHYD DDU & THE RANGER PATH

S From the car park, head past the public toilets. **Ignore** the sign for Snowdon and **bear slightly left**, back toward the main road. **Turn right** at the end of the road and go through the metal swing gate with *Snowdon Ranger* written on it. After 300m, take the **left fork**. The path from here is continuous but sometimes indistinct; there are frequent yellow and white marker posts to guide the way. You'll pass through the disused quarries and cross directly over the track which leads up to Llyn Ffynnon-y-gwas. The path rises gently over open moorland, passing through a wall before reaching the Snowdon Ranger Path.

2 **Turn right** on to the Ranger Path, climbing gradually up to the foot of the ridge which leads to the shoulder of Clogwyn Du'r Arddu. The path remains clear and easy to follow however the going gets tough. Climb steeply up the switchbacks, gaining height quickly. The path starts to bear right.

3 Cross the Snowdon Railway (**take care**), go straight over and **bear gently rightwards** to shortly reach the finger-stone which marks the top of the Pyg Track. Continue uphill with the railway to your right to the summit of Snowdon.

4 From the summit, head to the cafe and go down the slate steps adjacent to the entrance (the opposite way to your ascent). Initially the path descends some steep, rocky ground. Shortly after, as it levels, look for a large finger-stone inscribed with directions to Rhyd Ddu – **follow this**. The path runs along a narrow ridge for a short distance, swapping sides as you go.

5 Be careful to **bear right** following the fence line which runs above Llechog. The track is wide and easy to follow but rocky so **take care**. Pass through a gate, follow the path down and around to the **left**. There are some quite technical sections of rock before reaching a large, easy-going track. Follow the signs **right** to Rhyd Ddu. Take care crossing the railway and **turn left** back into the car park.

LOOKING ACROSS TO THE RIDGE OF CRIB GOCH FROM HIGH ON SNOWDON

STEVE FRANKLIN ON THE WALES COAST PATH

18 » NEWBOROUGH FOREST & BEACH   15.2km

INTRODUCTION

A delightfully flat route with spectacular views, mixed terrain and a nice break in the middle to explore the wonderful island of Ynys Llanddwyn. The old remains of a church can be found on the northern side of the island; this is the church of St Dwynwen – Llanddwyn means 'the church of St Dwynwen'. She is the Welsh patron saint of lovers, the English equivalent being St Valentine. On the western-most tip of Ynys Llanddwyn stands Twr Mawr lighthouse – with such an enticing path leading to its foot it's hard not to make the journey. The two large stone crosses seem to dominate the skyline of the island and these were erected by the island's then owner F.G. Wynn; both have inscriptions at their base.

This route is at its best later in the day as the sun is setting, when the mountains of Snowdonia are bathed in a spectacular light and look truly magnificent.

THE ROUTE

A wonderful run through the diverse Newborough Forest on to Ynys Llanddwyn and along the beach. While the forest can be disorientating in places, the route is made up of a number of waymarked routes which help with navigation. If the 15-kilometre loop is a little too far the route can be easily made shorter without missing out on the main events.

NB If you wish to visit the island of Ynys Llanddwyn then it's important to check the tide times as the island is cut off at high tide and you don't want to miss out!

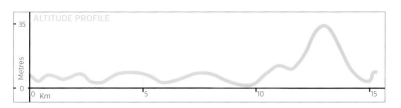

ALTITUDE PROFILE

Metres — 35 — 0

0 Km   5   10   15

» NEWBOROUGH FOREST & BEACH

DISTANCE 15.2KM » **ASCENT** 134M » **TYPICAL TIME** 1:45–2:30 HRS » **TERRAIN** ROAD/FIRE ROAD, TRAIL » **NAVIGATION** 1 – THE FOREST CAN BE DISORIENTATING SO A COMPASS IS USEFUL. HOWEVER, THE ROUTE IS COMPRISED OF A NUMBER OF MARKED ROUTES SO THERE ARE FREQUENT COLOURED WAYMARKERS [NOT ALL THE SAME COLOUR!] » **START/FINISH** FREE PARKING AT PEN COB CAR PARK » **GRID REF** SH 411671 » **SATNAV** LL61 6SH [NEAREST] » **OS MAP** EXPLORER 263 ANGLESEY EAST » **REFRESHMENTS** NONE AT PEN COB, CLOSEST NEWBOROUGH OR MALLTRAETH. PUBLIC TOILETS AT THE CAR PARK

TWR MAWR LIGHTHOUSE

N

Tyddyn

Hendre

Cefn
Maes-y-deirchir
Erw-wen

Llwyn
Bedigol

Dunes

Newborough Warren/
Tywyn Niwbwrch

Carreg-eithin

Bryn-Refail

Tir-mawr

Goeben

Hafoty

Gallt-rhedyn

Clwc-gwlyn

Newborough Warren and Ynys Llandd
National Nature Reserve

Penllyn Pysgod

Toll

4

Rhosydd

Mean High Water

Ro Fawr

Tir-Forgan

5

Cwrt

Craig Las

Traeth Llanddwyn

Crochan
Llanddwyn

Reservoir

P

Newborough Forest

65

Reservoir

63

69

Reservoirs

Dunes

Llanddwyn Bay

40

MLW

Cerrig-duon

Bryn-llwyd

Cadair
Cythrauli

Cerrig
mawr

Ro Bach

Ro Bach

Y Llanddwyn

3

Dunes
Wales Coast Path

2

Craig y
Ynys y Clochydd

Trwyn Ffynnon-y-Sais

Porth y Cwch

Llanddwyn Island/
Ynys Llanddwyn

Tower

Traeth Penrhos

Ffynnon Dafaden
(Spring)

Ynys-y-cranc

Ynys y Mochyn

orth y Dulas

Ynys yr Adar

S Go through the gate at the back of Pen Cob car park and follow the singletrack path for 100m and **turn right** down the wide trail. Stay on the trail, initially following the black 'Woodland Trot' waymarkers. **Turn right** just after 1.6km.* The track skirts the edge of the forest giving great views of Malltraeth Sands. Continue round to the headland of Ynys Llanddwyn.

*OPTIONAL ROUTE

OR After a further 1.6km there is an optional route: if the tide is low and you don't mind running on the sand then follow the green 'Dwynwen Heritage Walk' waymarkers. This route gives some more varied running and offers even more spectacular views of Malltraeth Sands.

2 As you approach Ynys Llanddwyn, pass **carefully** over the rocks which partially bridge the gap between the mainland and island. The island is best accessed from the southern side, next to a large noticeboard sign. **Please be aware dogs are not allowed on the island.** Once on the island explore at your will but make sure the tide isn't on the way in. Leave the island the same way you accessed it.

3 **Bear right** on to the beach; at low tide the beach is firm and easy to run on, at high tide it's not so easy (there are paths just off the beach within the forest which might be useful at very high tides). Run along the beach, past the wooden decking – this marks the main car park. Shortly after the decking at the edge of the forest, **turn left**, up through the sand dunes. After 50m there is a well-trodden path running the edge of the woodland – head along this keeping the fence on your right. **The most crucial turn** of the route is marked by a large, blue plastic bird box attached to a tree: **turn left** on to a 2m-wide path just after this.

4 Run through the narrow corridor to shortly reach a large track and a wooden post, marked with the number 36. **Turn right** on to the track and follow the waymarkers for the 'Corsica Trail'. The track loops gradually around to your left before joining the main road in and out of the forest. **Turn right** on to the road and at a house on your left **turn left** and then **right** just before the house gates.

5   Follow the path around to the right to reach a gate leading to an open field blocked by a bollard. **Turn left** heading gently uphill. At the next junction and a post marked '31' **turn right** down the hill, **bearing left** at the bottom. This path brings you out on the original track you entered the forest on. **Turn right** and retrace your outward route back to the start.

LOOKING ACROSS LLANDDWYN BAY TO SNOWDONIA

TONY WHITEHOUSE DESCENDING BACK TO CAPEL CURIG

19 ›› LLYN CRAFNANT & COWLYD RESERVOIR

16km

INTRODUCTION

The far end of the Crafnant valley is as spectacular as it is secluded. Reached by many by car from the Conwy valley, there are few better ways to access the valley than on foot from Capel Curig. At the head of the valley are the mountains of Crimpiau and Craig Wen, with the imposing rock face of Clogwyn yr Eryr on the northern slopes. The valley is perhaps not the largest or most dramatic in Wales, but it feels unbelievably remote and peaceful.

In the adjacent valley, the behemoth of a llyn which is the Cowlyd Reservoir comes as quite a contrast. It is the deepest of all the lakes in North Wales at seventy metres and is seemingly endless in length.

It feels quite moody and imposing, and the steep flanks on either side accentuate its grand nature. The Ogwen valley towards the end of the run feels like an open expanse in comparison.

THE ROUTE

While predominantly on open footpaths and tracks, this route has some technical sections both up and downhill and on rocky and very muddy terrain. The section after exiting the forest above Llyn Crafnant and descending down to the Cowlyd dam wall is a lot of fun but is often very wet.

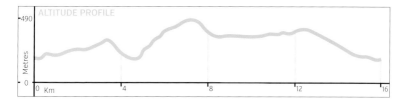

ALTITUDE PROFILE

›› **LLYN CRAFNANT & COWLYD RESERVOIR**

DISTANCE 16KM ›› *ASCENT* 340M ›› *TYPICAL TIME* 2:00–4:00 HRS ›› *TERRAIN* PATHS/TRODS, ROCKY/TECHNICAL ›› *NAVIGATION* 4 – NAVIGATION SKILLS ARE REQUIRED. ROUTE IS NEVER TOO EXPOSED BUT POOR NAVIGATION BETWEEN THE TWO LLYNS COULD LEAD INTO THE CONWY VALLEY ›› *START/FINISH* PAY & DISPLAY CAR PARK BEHIND JOE BROWNS SHOP IN CAPEL CURIG ›› *GRID REF* SH 720582 ›› *SATNAV* LL24 0EN ›› *OS MAP* EXPLORER OL17 SNOWDON ›› *TRANSPORT* REGULAR BUSES FROM BETHESDA, BETWS-Y-COED, LLANBERIS AND BEDDEGELERT ›› *REFRESHMENTS* CAFE, VILLAGE SHOP, PUBLIC TOILETS & JOE BROWNS OUTDOOR SHOP IN CAPEL CURIG

DIRECTIONS » LLYN CRAFNANT & COWLYD RESERVOIR

S From the car park head back to the T-junction. Cross the road and go through the gate opposite the shops. Run up the hill until you reach an oak tree, ford and bridge. Go over the bridge following the good path into the woods. Continue on this until you reach another bridge.

2 Cross the bridge and take the **left-hand fork**. Follow the rocky path through several gates and over several stiles. As the path starts to climb and shortly after passing the remnants of an old building take the **middle of the three paths, bearing gently left**.

3 The path starts to descend rapidly. If you dare risk taking your eyes off your feet, the views down the valley from here are fantastic. Keep descending the winding path until you reach a large gate at the head of Llyn Crafnant. Do not go through the gate but go **straight ahead/slight left** with the wall on your right (**do not** take the track immediately left towards the farm buildings). Cross the concrete bridge, go through the wooden gate and **bear right**. 5m before the next metal gate is a narrow path heading up into the forest, **take this**.

4 Follow the path uphill and cross another large concrete bridge. Immediately after the bridge take the small path on your **right**, following the yellow arrow. The path briefly follows the river before crossing it again via some rocky steps. As you climb up through the woods the route is marked by yellow arrows. **Keep your eyes peeled for the arrows** – you'll probably have your head down so don't forget to look up. You shouldn't run on the fire roads for any longer than a few hundred metres.

5 Eventually the path exits the forest via a wooden stile over a fence. Continue **straight ahead** along a narrow but quite well-trodden path (old fence posts help to mark it). Cross the large, wooden stile over the next fence. The path is faint from here to the dam wall but as long as you're going downhill you cannot miss it.

6   Run over the dam wall to the northern side of the reservoir. Take the path on your **left** with the water on your left. On reaching the far end of the reservoir, continue along the obvious path to reach a large wooden bridge and black swing gate. **Go through this.** Stay on the large path (bridleway), passing over several more wooden plank bridges. Once at Tal-y-waun farm, stay above the building and on the path to reach a stile and gate leading on to the A5. **Turn left** on to the narrow footpath which runs alongside the A5. **Please take care** along this stretch as the A5 can be busy. After about 800m you'll arrive back in Capel Curig.

CLIMBING ABOVE COWLYD RESERVOIR

KEITH SHARPLES HEADING INTO THE CARNEDDAU BACKCOUNTRY

INTRODUCTION

A magnificent tour of the northern Carnedds from the towering Aber Falls. This is not a run for the faint-hearted or those who don't like big climbs. This is very much a run of two halves – but while Carnedd Gwenllian marks the midpoint in terms of distance, it certainly doesn't in terms of time …

THE ROUTE

Don't be perturbed by the initial climb from Aber Falls car park, as when the North Wales Path reaches the plateau the views over Anglesey, Puffin Island and Llandudno are spectacular. The gradient eases off for a short distance before heading inland towards the summit of Drum. The path steepens but is runnable and easy underfoot. On a clear day a glance to your right reveals the journey ahead towards Moel Wnion and Drosgl.

Be sure to catch your breath as you descend off Drum as the pull up to Foel-fras isn't to be underestimated; with hands on knees keep on going and think of all the downhill that's to follow. It's from Foel-fras looking south that the summits of the Carneddau and Glyders become clear.

Take care with your navigation from Foel-fras to Gwenllian, and most importantly from Gwenllian heading west down to Drosgl. The ground is rough for a short distance but soon opens out again as the trods turn to trails. A very short and gentle uphill takes you on to the flanks of Moel Wnion. Take a minute and look right towards the giant Aber Falls waterfall. Alas, just when you think you're back at the start, a small dogleg is required to drop back down to the road; maybe think of it as a gentle warm down.

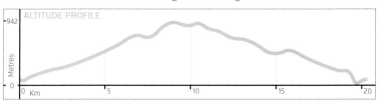

ALTITUDE PROFILE

942

Metres

0

0 Km   5   10   15   20

>> **NORTHERN CARNEDDAU**

DISTANCE 20.4KM >> *ASCENT* 970M >> *TYPICAL TIME* 2:30–5:00 HRS >> *TERRAIN* ROCKY/TECHNICAL, OPEN FELL OR HANDS ON >> *NAVIGATION* 4 – QUITE EASY TO NAVIGATE IN CLEAR VISIBILITY. IF VISIBILITY IS POOR, FINDING THE RIGHT LINE OFF CARNEDD GWENLLIAN TOWARDS BERA BACH AND DROSGL IS VERY DIFFICULT. REMEMBER, VISIBILITY HIGH UP CAN BE MARKEDLY DIFFERENT TO SEA LEVEL >> *START/FINISH* PAY & DISPLAY AT ABER FALLS >> *GRID REF* SH 662720 >> *SATNAV* LL33 0LP >> *OS MAP* EXPLORER OL17 SNOWDON >> *TRANSPORT* BUSES OFF A55 TO ABERGWYNGREGYN >> *REFRESHMENTS* CAFE HEN FELIN, ABERGWYNGREGYN TEL: 01248 689 454

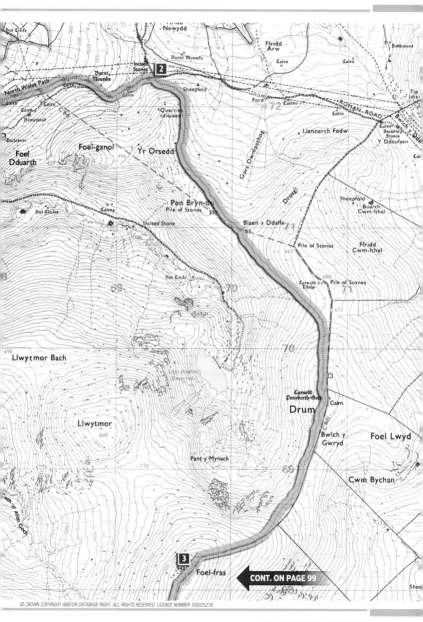

North Wales Path

Foel Dduarth

Foel-ganol

Yr Orsedd

Frydd Newydd

Ffrydd Arw

Incised Stones **2**

Burnt Mounds

Cairn

Cairn

Settlement

Burnt Mounds

Sheepfold

Ford

Cairns

ROMAN ROAD

72

Bwlch y Ddeufaen

Standing Stones

Y Ddeufaen

Tip (dis)

Llannerch Fedw

Quarries (disused)

Gors Drumpathog

Drosgl

Sheepfold

Buarth Cwm-Ithel

Pen Bryn-du Pile of Stones

Blaen y Ddalfa BS.

Pile of Stones

Ffrydd Cwm-Ithel

Incised Stone

Hut Circles

Cairns

Hut Circle

69

70

Carnedd Ddelw

Pile of Stones

71

Llwytmor Bach

690

Llyn Anafon (Reservoir)

Llwytmor

849

70

Carnedd Penyborth-Goch

Drum

Cairn

Bwlch y Gwryd

Foel Lwyd

Pant y Mynach

776

69

Cwm Bychan

Cwm yr Afon Goch

3

Foel-fras

CONT. ON PAGE 99

Shee

DIRECTIONS >> NORTHERN CARNEDDAU

S From the car park, cross over the bridge. **Do not** take the path to Aber Falls but carry on along the road. It's a tough start up the road but stick with it. Climb steeply until you reach another car park and the road head. **Turn left**, keeping next to the drystone wall. Continue along this path until you're underneath the large pylon cables and **turn right** on to the North Wales Path.

2 Run along the North Wales Path until you reach a definitive crossroads with a signpost. **Turn right** following the sign to *Drum*. The track remains wide and well trodden so is easy to follow. The route does fork for a short distance, however both routes reconvene so take either path. It climbs gradually until the path draws alongside a fence line. Start to climb more steeply as you head up to the summit of Drum. From the summit continue along the path using the fence line as a reference. It's a little wet under foot. There's one last push up Foel-Fras; shortly before the summit the fence changes to stone wall.

3 From the trig point, head back to the path running adjacent to the wall. After 500m the wall line turns sharply leftwards and the path bears off right; **follow the path right**. Descend gradually to a plateau marked by a finger-stone with the letters *RWB* inscribed in it. **Go straight on**, as the path starts to ascend you'll pass another finger-stone with the same inscription. The path peters out as you head towards the summit of Carnedd Gwenllian. The summit is nondescript and is marked by a large rocky tor. There is no trig point and in poor visibility it's difficult to ascertain whether you're at the summit or not.

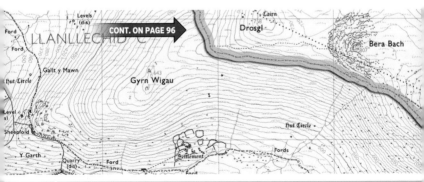

CONT. ON PAGE 96

4   If in doubt, from the rocky tor move on a bearing of 291°. The path descends through rocky patches, passing several small pools of water. **Be careful not to lose height too quickly.** If visibility is good, head towards the two very prominent rocky summits of Bera Mawr and Bera Bach, aiming just to the left of Bera Bach. The path contours to the south of Bera Bach on a narrow trod. Drop steeply off Bera Bach to a plateau before contouring around the southern border of Drosgl. South-west of Drosgl the path becomes more obvious, turning to track once again. Continue down along the wide path until you reach a small cairn and path junction.

5   **Turn right** at the cairn; the path is narrow and rises very gently on to the eastern side of Moel Wnion. As the slope to your right becomes less steep, keep an eye out for a small path heading towards the electricity pylons. Descend until you're stood beneath the pylons and **turn right** on to the path. Follow this to the wall and **turn right** again (back on yourself). After 400m cross the wall at a large wooden stile and **bear left** heading diagonally down the field to reach a wide track. **Turn left** on the track, through a gate. At the junction with the North Wales Path, **turn right**, steeply downhill. Don't get carried away and keep your eyes peeled for a narrow path on your **right** which takes you back to the road. Go through the metal swing gate and **turn right** on to the road for a nice cool down back to the car park.

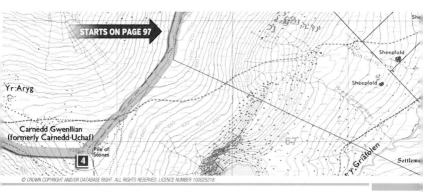

STEVE FRANKLIN ON THE WELL-SURFACED TRAILS AT COED Y BRENIN

Bonus Section >> COED Y BRENIN

INTRODUCTION

Coed y Brenin is Natural Resources Wales' premier recreational site: there is something for everyone here. The breadth of activities available within Coed y Brenin is what makes it. Whether you mountain bike, run, like arts and crafts, want to go on a gentle stroll, love coffee and cake, or want to keep the kids busy while doing any of the above you're at the ideal place!

The main features of Coed y Brenin are the mountain bike trails and bike hire centre, an amazing children's adventure playground, the Animal Puzzle Trail and, most importantly, Run Coed y Brenin – the UK's first bespoke trail running centre.

In addition to all of this, the visitor centre is open seven days a week and has a fantastic set of facilities, including a cafe (with an extensive local menu), accessible toilets, baby changing facilities, showers, a shop and information point.

Information about the centre and the plethora of activities available can be found online, in addition to on the noticeboards on site.

RUN COED Y BRENIN

Of particular interest to readers of this book is Run Coed y Brenin, the UK's first bespoke trail running centre. There's a well-stocked shop, demo shoes for hire and access to a variety of waymarked trails through spectacular woodland and mountain scenery. The trails range from 4.3 kilometres through to 22 kilometres, and it's easy to mix and match if you're short of time or want to go a little further.

If you're lucky your trip might coincide with one of the many events held at Run CyB. There are a number of races during the year as well as talks and guided night runs.

GETTING THERE

Coed y Brenin is located in the south of Snowdonia National Park, on the A470 just north of Dolgellau. Although not located in very close proximity to some of the more popular areas, it's an hour's drive from Llanberis in the north, Aberystwth in the south and Welshpool in the east.

>> COED Y BRENIN

GRID REF SH 723268 >> *SATNAV* LL40 2HZ >> *FACILITIES* EVERYTHING! >> *MORE INFORMATION* WWW.RUNCOEDYBRENIN.COM

≫ APPENDIX

The following is a list of Tourist Information Centres, shops, cafes, pubs, websites and other contacts that might come in handy.

TOURIST INFORMATION CENTRES

North Wales Tourism .... www.gonorthwales.co.uk

Snowdonia Tourism ..... www.visitsnowdonia.info

Official website of **Snowdonia National Park** .... www.eryri-npa.gov.uk

Aberdyfi, Wharf Gardens (Easter–Oct)
T 01654 767 321 .. **E** tic.aberdyfi@eryri-npa.gov.uk

Beddgelert, Canolfan Hebog (Easter–Oct)
T 01766 890 615.. **E** tic.beddgelert@eryri-npa.gov.uk

Betws-y-Coed, Royal Oak Stables
T 01690 710 426 .... **E** tic.byc@eryri-npa.gov.uk

Conwy, Castle Building
T 01492 592 248 .... **E** conwytic@conwy.gov.uk

Llandudno, Library Building, Mostyn Street
T 01492 577 577 .... **E** llandudnotic@conwy.gov.uk

Mold, Earl Road
T 01352 759 331 .... **E** mold@nwtic.com

FOOD AND DRINK

CAFES
(See individual routes for recommendations.)

Caffi'r Parc, Breakwater Country Park
T 01407 760 530 .... www.caffirparc.org.uk

Cafe Hen Felin, Abergwyngregyn .. **T** 01248 689 454

Pete's Eats, Llanberis .... **T** 01286 870 117
www.petes-eats.co.uk

Caffi Sam, Llanberis .... **T** 07746 831 127

Caffi Gwynant, Nant Gwynant .... **T** 01766 890 855
www.cafesnowdon.co.uk

Caffi Caban Cafe, Brynrefail .... **T** 01286 685 500
www.caban-cyf.org

Lodge Dinorwig, Dinorwig .... **T** 01286 871 632

Caban Café, Pen-y-Pass .... **T** 01286 870 500

Ogwen Cottage Cafe (summer only)

Moel Siabod Cafe, Capel Curig .. **T** 01690 720 429
www.moelsiabodcafe.co.uk

Oriel Caffi Croesor at Cnicht .... **T** 01766 771 433

Lakeside Cafe, Tanygrisiau .... **T** 01766 830 950

Llyn Brenig Visitor Centre Cafe ... **T** 01490 420 463
www.llyn-brenig.co.uk

Caffi Meinir, Nant Gwrtheyrn .... **T** 01758 750 442
www.nantgwrtheyrn.org

Tŷ Te Cadair Tea Room, Minffordd .. **T** 01654 761 505

PUBS
(See individual routes for recommendations.)

Cwellyn Arms, Rhyd Ddu .... **T** 01766 890 321
www.snowdoninn.co.uk

Vaynol Arms, Nant Peris .... **T** 01286 872 672

The Heights, Llanberis .... **T** 01286 238 235
www.theheightsllanberis.co.uk

Bryn Tyrch Inn, Capel Curig ...... **T** 01690 720 223
www.bryntyrchinn.co.uk

We Three Loggerheads, Loggerheads
T 01352 810 337 .. www.we-three-loggerheads.co.uk

Cross Foxes, Brithdir, Nr Dolgellau
T 01341 421 001 .... www.crossfoxes.co.uk

Y Giler Arms, Nr Betws-y-Coed .. **T** 01690 770 612
www.giler.co.uk

ACCOMMODATION

YOUTH HOSTELS
YHA Youth Hostels can be found in the following places. For more information please visit www.yha.org.uk

Betws-y-Coed .... **T** 01690 710 796
Conwy .... **T** 0345 371 9732
Idwal .... **T** 0345 371 9744
Kings (Dolgellau) .... **T** 0345 371 9327
Snowdon Bryn Gwynant .... **T** 0345 371 9108
Snowdon Llanberis .... **T** 0345 371 9645
Snowdon Pen-y-Pass .... **T** 0345 371 9534
Snowdon Ranger .... **T** 0345 371 9659

BUNKHOUSES, B&BS AND HOTELS
www.gonorthwales.co.uk
For specific information, contact a Tourist Information Centre in the area in which you intend to stay.

BUNKHOUSES
Jesse James Bunkhouse, Caernarfon
T 01286 870 521 .... www.jessejamesbunkhouse.co.uk

Pete's Eats Bunkhouse, Llanberis
T 01286 870 117 .... www.petes-eats.co.uk

CAMPING
Tyisaf Campsite, Nant Peris .... **T** 01286 870 494

Y Giler Arms, Nr Betws-y-Coed .. **T** 01690 770 612
www.giler.co.uk

Beddgelert Camping in the Forest
T 0845 130 8224 .... www.campingintheforest.co.uk
There are many, more campsites in North Wales – try www.coolcamping.co.uk or www.gonorthwales.co.uk

WEATHER
www.metoffice.gov.uk
www.mwis.org.uk

RUNNING & OUTDOOR SHOPS
Run Shop Run, Coed y Brenin
T 01341 440 798 . . . . *www.runshoprun.co.uk*

Cotswold Outdoor, Betws-y-Coed
T 01690 348 316/01690 348 261
www.cotswoldoutdoor.com

V12 Outdoor, Llanberis
T 01286 871 534 . . . . *www.v12outdoor.com*

Joe Browns, Llanberis
T 01286 870 327 . . . . *www.joe-brown.com*

Joe Brown, Capel Curig
T 01690 720 205 . . . . *www.joe-brown.com*

Up & Running, Chester
T 01244 345 812 . . . . *www.upandrunning.co.uk*

OTHER PUBLICATIONS
Peak District Trail Running
Nikalas Cook & Jon Barton
Vertebrate Publishing
www.v-publishing.co.uk

Lake District Trail Running
Helen Mort
Vertebrate Publishing
www.v-publishing.co.uk

Good Run Guide
Louise Piears & Andy Bickerstaff
Vertebrate Publishing
www.v-publishing.co.uk

Day Walks in Snowdonia
Tom Hutton
Vertebrate Publishing
www.v-publishing.co.uk

Wales Mountain Biking
Tom Hutton
Vertebrate Publishing
www.v-publishing.co.uk

AT THE SUMMIT OF YR EIFL » RUN 8
PHOTO JON BARTON

ABOUT THE AUTHOR

A relative latecomer to the sport, **Steve Franklin** started running after a rock climbing injury left him unable to climb. He set the bar high with the aim of beating his brother's Iron Man marathon time (three hours and ten minutes) but stupidly chose the Snowdon Marathon, the nearest one to his then home in Bangor, North Wales, to make the bid. Needless to say he failed, completing the marathon in three hours and twenty-one minutes. Since that fateful day Steve has left the tarmac and ventured on to the fells. He now lives in Sheffield where he owns and runs a running shop (Front Runner). He regularly heads back to North Wales for extended trips to run and climb, and in 2014 he completed the Paddy Buckley Round (104 kilometres and 8,500 metres of ascent and descent in under twenty-four hours).
www.frontrunnersheffield.co.uk

ABOUT THE PHOTOGRAPHER

Keith Sharples has been lugging camera kit around the four corners of the globe (is that possible?) for decades. Originally a climbing photographer, Keith's interest has diversified in later years and now includes other outdoor sports such as running. Let's face it; photographing runners is a heck of a lot easier than running yourself – right? The routes around North Wales are through such stunning scenery it's hard not to get psyched and slip into your running kit for a cheeky potter when the sun's out.
www.keithsharplesphotography.co.uk

ABOUT VERTEBRATE PUBLISHING

At Vertebrate Publishing we publish books to inspire adventure.

It's our rule that the only books we publish are those that we'd want to read or use ourselves. We endeavour to bring you beautiful books that stand the test of time and that you'll be proud to have on your bookshelf for years to come. The Peak District was the inspiration behind our first books. Our offices are situated on its doorstep, minutes away from world-class climbing, biking and hillwalking. We're driven by our own passion for the outdoors, for exploration, and for the natural world; it's this passion that we want to share with our readers.

We aim to inspire everyone to get out there. We want to connect readers – young and old – with the outdoors and the positive impact it can have on well-being. We think it's particularly important that young people get outside and explore the natural world, something we support through our publishing programme.

As well as publishing award-winning new books, we're working to make available many out-of-print classics in both print and digital formats. These are stories that we believe are unique and significant; we want to make sure that they continue to be shared and enjoyed.
www.v-publishing.co.uk

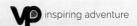

inspiring adventure

Good Run
Guide

The *Good Run Guide* features 40 of the most scenic runs in England and Wales. Ranging in length from 3.4 to 10.7 miles (5.4 to 17.2 kilometres), there are routes for runners of all ability and fitness levels, on a range of surfaces.

Written by experienced runners Louise Piears and Andy Bickerstaff, founders of the Good Run Guide, the UK's leading independent running website, it is an essential glovebox companion for trips away in England and Wales.

Find out more and order direct: **www.v-publishing.co.uk**

Fancy some more trail and fell running?

PEAK DISTRICT
» TRAIL RUNNING
22 OFF-ROAD ROUTES FOR TRAIL & FELL RUNNERS

LAKE DISTRICT
» TRAIL RUNNING
20 OFF-ROAD ROUTES FOR TRAIL & FELL RUNNERS

- Ordnance Survey 1:25,000 maps • easy-to-follow directions
- details of distance and timings • refreshment stops • local knowledge

Find out more and order direct at **www.v-publishing.co.uk**

 inspiring adventure